PIZZA

THE DISH, THE LEGEND

PIZZA
THE DISH, THE LEGEND

Rosario Buonassisi

FIREFLY BOOKS

A FIREFLY BOOK

Published by Firefly Books Ltd. 2000
First published in Italian as *Pizze e Non Pizze: Una breve storia della pizza dal neolitico ai giorni nostri* by Arnoldo Mondadori Editore, S.p.A.

First Printing

U.S. Cataloging-in-Publication Data

Buonassisi, Rosario
   Pizza : from Italian origins to the modern table / Rosario Buonassisi. — 1st ed.
[168]p. : col. ill. ; cm.
Summary: A history of pizza plus the best Italian pizza recipes.
ISBN 1-55209-321-2 (pbk.)
1. Pizza. 2. Pizza — Italy. I. Title.
641.8/ 24   2000   CIP

Canadian Cataloguing in Publication Data

Buonassisi, Rosario
   Pizza : from its Italian origins to the modern table

Translation of: La pizza : il piatto, la leggenda.
Includes index.
ISBN 1-55209-321-2

1. Pizza. I. Title.

TX770.P58B8613   2000   641.8'24   C00-930874-1

Published in Canada in 2000 by
Firefly Books Ltd.
3680 Victoria Park Avenue
Willowdale, Ontario
M2H 3KI

Published in the United States in 2000 by
Firefly Books (U.S.) Inc.
P.O. Box 1338, Ellicott Station
Buffalo, New York
14205

Printed and bound in Spain
D.L. TO: 391 - 2000

A special acknowledgment is due to Nazir Lewiz, owner of the pizzeria OK Campione di Milano, who prepared all of the pizzas in the recipe section. Photographs of the recipes in the second chapter: Maj-Britt Idström.

Contents

$\mathscr{I}$NTRODUCTION

Rosario! You call that a pizza?

The first problem that I encountered when I began this book was how to decide exactly what is a pizza. That may sound silly, but it is not. Almost every traditional cuisine on earth features dishes that could be construed as cousins to the pizza, however many times removed. Some of them are princely cousins—such as the Russian blini, accustomed to the company of caviar—while others are humbler relatives, such as the Indian chapati, a simple thin flatbread eaten with vegetables and boiled pulses. Curry is often used in an attempt to ennoble this combination.

There are plenty of other doughy cousins of the pizza. They extend over the world in an intricate and endless family tree and include the calzone of Italy—which some aficionados consider to be a particularly rich pizza folded over on itself before being slipped into the oven to bake. There's even a real affinity between the Arab shawarma and the calzone. To complicate matters still further, in some cases the same name is used to describe radically different dishes. In Naples "pizza" is a term that can describe either the classic Neapolitan pizza (and its various first cousins), or a portion of leavened dough, fried in oil, and eaten plain or smeared or even stuffed with ricotta cheese, eggs, and salami. In the city of Rome, on the other hand, "pizza" has always meant a leavened bread dough, loosely rolled out to uneven thicknesses, and flavored only with oil and salt. This time-honored recipe, of which more will be said, may be thought of as the missing link between pizza and focaccia.

Pizza—a definition

When trying to define pizza, one sets out on a sea of troubles. And though these apparently idle musings on the exact definition of pizza may seem insignificant compared with deeper questions about existence, to food-loving persons such as myself they are of crucial importance. The history of food is an integral part of the history of humanity. So let's give pizza its due. Let us look for its humble beginnings and trace its long life to the present, where it has almost become its own food group. But that is rushing ahead. We shall begin humbly. And what's more humble than a rather arid and technical definition? It will help us discuss both the Neapolitan pizza—pizza par excellence—and its many lesser but still delicious cousins scattered all over the world. My definition runs as follows:

Pizza: a thin layer of leavened dough, ideally disk-shaped, made by thoroughly kneading wheat flour, yeast, salt, olive oil, and water and then covering with various ingredients before being baked in an oven. The different ingredients employed determine the taste and smell—and the name—of the various kinds of pizza.

In this book, I will use pizza both as a term for the entire broad category and for individual varieties of pizza. Note that I specify the thin layer of dough, the crust, that typifies pizza in the original Italian style; this is very different from the thick-crusted, deep-dish creations that many call pizza, but which in fact is not the real thing.

Admittedly, such definitions and specifications would not be out of place in a patent office, but they are meant to eliminate ambiguity and ward off potential confusion with any of the other treasures of Italian regional cuisine. Technical terminology, however, is entirely inadequate to describe the superb culinary qualities of pizza that have made this ancient and popular dish the favorite food of Italy and a symbol of Italian cuisine around the globe.

In praise of pizza

Though pizza may have originally developed as an inexpensive foodstuff to feed the poor of certain parts of Italy, it remains a masterpiece of Italian folk cuisine. The very sound of the word "pizza" is enough to conjure up gratifying memories of delicious and robust flavors and aromas that even an untrained, unrefined palate cannot fail to instinctively appreciate. The very first bite brings an irresistible flood of bracing flavors—each enhancing the others. Certain pungent tastes, such as the anchovies in the classic Neapolitan pizza, are immediately softened and absorbed by the sensual flavor of mozzarella. Atop this blend of tastes, skillfully applied tomatoes and olive oil add a crowning touch.

The taste may vary slightly from one variety to another, but pizzas always start from the simple and age-old flavor of the crust, the cornerstone in the culinary architecture of every pizza. The crust has a full-bodied flavor, but not overwhelming, characterized by fundamentally sweet highlights, with the bracing counterpoint of the shifting, bitterish flavors of the edge. (This raised edge is not protected by the toppings, so it becomes slightly charred in spots by the intense heat of the oven.) Underneath the

toppings and above the bottom surface, which in contact with the oven becomes delightfully crisp, the crust retains the springy, chewy texture of dense, fresh bread. What makes a pizza still more alluring is the perfectly balanced combination of varied aromas. Inevitably present is the delicate, vaguely ethereal perfume of the yeast in the dough, a perfect springboard for the more pronounced aromas of the various ingredients that range from the rustic to the refined and never fail to whet the appetite.

Pizza reaches beyond the senses of taste and smell, playing pleasurably upon the gift of sight. One can scarcely help feeling an immediate surge of joy upon seeing that bubbling disk, with its cheerful warm colors, revealing here and there the varied shades of the dough, with hues that range from gray to a light Naples yellow, framed by the short, sharp, dark brushstrokes where the outermost layer of crust is charred from the oven's heat. I'm not saying that every pizza chef is a visual artist, but the fact remains that the pleasure we gain through our taste buds from a well-made pizza is nicely enhanced by the shapes and colors—harmonious but haphazard, and always surprising—that greet our eye when the baker's shovel, or peel, extracts the pizza from the oven.

A dish for every meal, a food for every table

To grasp its widespread appeal, the pizza must be understood in more than purely gastronomic terms. A distinctive feature of the pizza is what I like to call its versatility, a characteristic that has contributed greatly to its growth in popularity around the globe. A pizza constitutes on its own, or with a salad, an excellent meal, whether lunch or dinner: quick, light, nutritious and healthful. It's a meal that fits perfectly into the description of the "Mediterranean diet," praised by dieticians the world over. It's perfect for those who can take but brief respite from their workday to eat. Among other things, it is worth noting that the habit of eating pizza at lunch was common in the United States many years before it became customary in Italy. (Evidence can be found in a detective story published in the late 1950s and set in New York City. The killer is identified by the fingerprints he left on the still-warm

mozzarella on a slice of pizza he was eating for lunch; when the time came to commit the murder, he tossed the slice of pizza aside and forgot about it.)

Pizza also offers an excellent opportunity for cheerful social gatherings among friends. What could be nicer than sharing a pizza, with a glass or two of fine wine? "Farsi una pizza assieme," or, "let's have ourselves a pizza"—as a fine old Italian phrase would have it—represents a form of togetherness that seems designed to solidify old friendships and create new ones. Particularly in Italy, but in other parts of the world too, pizza is traditionally eaten with the hands, in a series of physical actions as old as the earliest of peoples breaking bread together. A pizzeria, perhaps because of its informality, may also be an ideal place for that tentative first date—in an atmosphere warmed by the yellow flares of the wood fire burning in the oven, the smoldering red glow of the coals, and the sense of camaraderie in the air. First you wait to see the pizzas taken glistening and smoking from the black mouth of the oven. Next comes the communal meal. When you think that pizza is prepared today with techniques that have miraculously survived the passage of millennia, you understand that this dish is truly part of a timeless ritual.

An age-old tradition

There is an ancient magic in pizza and the ways it is prepared, but there is also a level-headed practicality that our jaded and modern sensibilities may fail to appreciate. A pizza chef will take a ball of leavened dough, flatten it with his or her hands, and then toss it spinning into the air, causing it to take on a disk shape with a slightly thicker border, or lip; this isn't done to show off juggling skills, but to take advantage of the centrifugal force that transforms the dough, delicately, without excessive pressure, from a sphere into a disk. The chef is following a tradition that was begun perhaps thousands of years ago. This is the only method which can produce a pizza that truly deserves the name. As for the "lip"—that raised edge of the crust—it actually has a dual function. First,

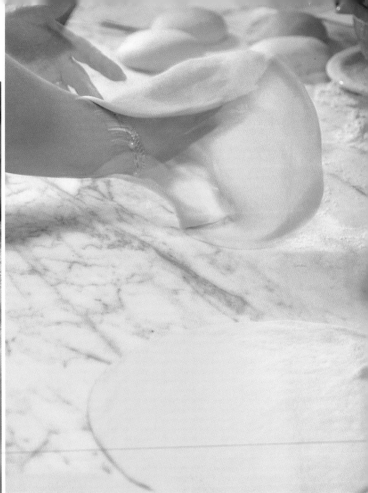

Some steps in the preparing
of pizza

it prevents the olive oil and any liquids that may form during the baking from dripping away when the pizza chef's shovel moves the pizza in the oven or brings it piping hot to the table. (Moving the pizza while baking does more than just allow the pizza to bake evenly; it also helps to distribute the liquids evenly over the surface. So the crust remains soft, despite the intense heat of the oven. At the same time the aromatic agents, such as garlic, oregano, and basil, which dissolve in the olive oil, are evenly distributed.) Second, the lip gives the pizza a certain rigidity, which for those of us who still eat it on the street, makes it possible to consume a slice without too much risk of losing the contents. Finally, the lip provides what engineers call a "rigid breaking point," facilitating the division of a pizza into manageable slices.

The continuing use of wood-burning ovens in true pizzerias is not merely an attempt to preserve a folk tradition or to re-create a quaint old-world atmosphere. There is, in fact, a culinary principle involved. However dry the firewood and however good the draft, the interior of the oven will always have a little smoke inside, which will contribute a very slight but distinctive aroma and taste to the pizza. No matter how much pride a pizza chef takes in keeping the oven scrupulously clean, there is no way to prevent a microscopic layer of ash from adhering to the bottom surface of the pizza. This ash, in minimal quantities (totally harmless to the body), actually enhances—along with the salt in the crust—the crust's flavor. In various parts of Europe as late as the end of the eighteenth century, in fact, when salt was still a luxury, the poorer classes used to salt their foods with a mixture of salt and ashes from a wood fire, or, when poverty was extreme, with ashes alone.

Pizza today and tomorrow

Thanks to its incredible growth in many countries, and also because of considerable improvements in food preservation, pizza has attracted the interest of major retailers and food manufacturers. The convenience pizza market has also zoomed in recent decades. In many of the pizza chains and in

**Wood-burning ovens in
Neapolitan pizzerias**

supermarkets, after a long period in which the products sold were mainly glorified focaccia, you can now find genuine pizza. Some offerings are every bit as good as those made in a full-fledged pizzeria. However, the widespread success of these products could end up having a negative effect on the culinary characteristics of pizza. Why? Because a true pizza is unquestionably a matter of intuition and inspiration, at times falling just short of pure genius, that give constant change to a food that has long existed in the folk cuisine of central and southern Italy. A good pizza will mirror the personality of the pizza chef, and, in a certain sense, that of the diner, as long as that diner is offered an adequate array of pizzas from which to choose. In other words, the same pizza, prepared with the same ingredients by two pizza chefs, will have definite differences—the result of an individual interpretation of a recipe. The personality and the training of the pizza chef will also determine what sorts of pizza are offered on a menu. These differences and choices will, in turn, influence the preferences of the public.

On the other hand, mass-produced, ready-to-eat foods cannot, by definition, allow for variations in flavor, aroma, and appearance. Also, such items tend to make use of a limited number of ingredients. As a result, mass-produced pizza— some of it of admittedly acceptable quality, and often faithful to the traditional recipe—will always be characterized by a certain sameness and will offer consumers only a limited selection. There may well be differences from one manufacturer to another, but they are always minimal differences, because the recipes used—in terms of the proportions of the ingredients—are inevitably the product of rigorous market research, designed to appeal to the preferences (and preconceptions) of the largest possible number of consumers.

The danger in this situation is that, with the passage of time, consumers exposed to these prod-

**The Neapolitan singer
Aurelio Fierro puts a pizza
in the oven, Naples, 1955**

ucts may very well lose their desire for new and unexpected flavors. Now these products—and I intentionally use the term "products" to underscore the trend toward depersonalization—are often perfectly adequate in culinary terms. But over a shorter or longer period of time, the phenomenon of standardizing tastes will wind up affecting the behavior of pizza chefs as well: in the face of smaller demand for different types of pizza and a general preference for standardized qualities of flavor, aroma, and appearance, chefs will have little alternative but to comply with the demands of their clientele. The larger result of such a development would be a full-fledged stasis in the evolution of pizza as a whole. When a food or a dish enters a phase of that sort, it inevitably winds up losing those characteristics that constitute what I venture to call its "personality."

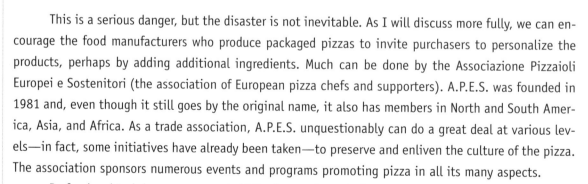

This is a serious danger, but the disaster is not inevitable. As I will discuss more fully, we can encourage the food manufacturers who produce packaged pizzas to invite purchasers to personalize the products, perhaps by adding additional ingredients. Much can be done by the Associazione Pizzaioli Europei e Sostenitori (the association of European pizza chefs and supporters). A.P.E.S. was founded in 1981 and, even though it still goes by the original name, it also has members in North and South America, Asia, and Africa. As a trade association, A.P.E.S. unquestionably can do a great deal at various levels—in fact, some initiatives have already been taken—to preserve and enliven the culture of the pizza. The association sponsors numerous events and programs promoting pizza in all its many aspects.

Professional training courses are held for future pizza chefs—not only to teach them how to prepare impeccable pizzas, but also to educate them on the meaning of the culture of pizza. Above all, however, A.P.E.S. has the potential to serve as intermediary with the food industry to find a balance between the economic benefits of standardization and the preservation of the oldest of traditions.

A little advice

Before ending this brief introduction, let me add one last thing. In the second chapter of this book I offer some recipes for various types of pizza, and I have also indicated the amount of each ingredient, based on what A.P.E.S. recommends in its training courses for pizza chefs. These measurements will allow you to achieve—your home oven permitting—the same culinary results that are so pleasing when we dine out in a pizzeria. The quantities, nonetheless, should be considered as suggestions really. When you prepare a pizza, give free rein to your personal tastes and your own sense of creativity. At first you may make a few mistakes, but in the end your imaginative impulses will have contributed to keeping alive the tradition and the culture of pizza.

PIZZAS AND

NON-PIZZAS

OR, A BRIEF HISTORY OF PIZZA

1

66 The history of pizza

is closely bound up

with the history of bread,

and therefore has

its earliest beginnings

somewhere in

the southeast

Mediterranean region . . .

PIZZAS & NON-PIZZAS
OR, A BRIEF HISTORY OF PIZZA

The earliest beginnings

The history of pizza is closely bound up with the history of bread, and therefore has its earliest beginnings somewhere in the southeast Mediterranean region, sometime between the twelfth and the third millennia BC. The late Neolithic era was witness to great transformations in human culture, and during this long period humanity was slowly turning from hunting wild animals to breeding livestock, from gathering plants to farming crops. In the same general period, humans invented pottery that could both hold water and withstand flame. Among the fundamentals of their daily diet were grains—barley, oats, or spelt—that humans had learned to plant, cultivate, and harvest. Spelt is a "dressed" grain; its kernel is surrounded by "glume," a tough, inedible, chafflike film; the spelt must first be roasted to loosen the covering that is then largely eliminated by grinding the kernels. And it was probably while grinding off the glume and eliminating it, that someone realized that if the kernels were ground between two stones for a good long time they turned into a rough powder, the earliest flour, which could be blended with water or milk, creating a nutritious mush.

Humanity has also known, for something like 300,000 years, that foods become tastier and easier to digest when exposed to the heat of a flame, and that cooked foods keep longer. It is only logical, then, to assume that someone must have begun to test the effects of cooking on those primitive mushes as well. Archeological evidence shows that watery mushes were cooked in earthenware pots. The result was what the modern Italian would term a "farinata," or wheat cake—early ancestors of the "pultes" and the "tisanae" of the ancient Romans, and the polenta and grits of the present. In other preparations, less liquid was used and a proper dough was made with the consistency of an elastic mass. This ball of dough was then flattened so that the heat could penetrate it in a uniform manner. It was then placed on a flat white-hot stone, or tucked under the ashes, or else set in terra-cotta molds and buried beneath the flames of the hearth.

This was the earliest of breads. First it took the unleavened form of relatively thin cakes or flatbreads, and—only rarely—round loaves. It was often prepared with barley, which was preferred over spelt because it was cheaper, though less nutritious. The resulting cakes were dense and compact. This way of preparing bread survived right up to historical times, as evidenced by the "maza" of archaic Greece and the cakes of barley bread mentioned in the Old Testament (*Judges* 7: 13).

With the passage of time, bread—though still unleavened—continued to evolve and improve in quality.

As the more thorough elimination of the chaff was made possible by better milling technology, finer flours were produced. This led to more consistent doughs. Often oils or animal fats were added, making the doughs more elastic and easier to knead. As a result, bread could be baked in different shapes: alongside the round loaves and the "focaccias," there were flatbreads of surprising thinness. Breads were baked for special occasions—banquets in honor of important guests, or as sacrificial offerings to the gods. Bread was further enriched by serving it with olive oil or even melted grease as a spread.

We have priceless documentation of these early recipes in the form of several ancient texts. Among these sources are the Holy Scriptures that, in the Old Testament, set forth the ceremonies with which the consecration of new priests was celebrated, stating among other things: "Take . . . unleavened bread, unleavened cakes mixed with oil, and unleavened wafers spread with oil. . . . And you shall put them in one basket" (*Exodus* 29: 1-3). There are also the famous *tabulae Iguvinae*, or Tables of Iguvium (modern Gubbio in the central Italian province of Umbria). The tables are liturgies in ancient Italic dialects engraved on sheets of bronze. Compiled sometime in the second half of the first millennium BC but apparently referring to a period prior to 700 BC, they set forth ancient Umbrian

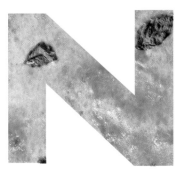

rituals and ceremonies. From them we learn, for instance, that sacrificial cakes had to be round in shape. These cakes were called "orfetas," a term that we may translate as "wheels," and were  often associated with "persondro," or grease, which appears variously in liquid and in solid form, though it is not clear whether the "persondro" was meant to be spread upon the "orfetas" or if it was offered separately. (Only the Old Testament calls for votive cakes to be exclusively unleavened. Apart from Judaism, this requirement is not found among those ancient religions whose rituals called for baked cereal cakes or loaves.)

The documentation is fragmentary and incomplete, but clearly shows that at the very dawn of recorded history humans were mixing flour, water, and olive oil to prepare cakes of bread dough that were probably sprinkled with more oil before being baked. These were ritual foods, but they were also daily staples, and it is in the context of how they were prepared and eaten that we can consider them as proto-pizza.

Aside from cakes, very thin forms of bread also were prepared, especially when wheat was used instead of barley. These thin breads were often baked a second time to dry them and facilitate their storage. This was unleavened bread, typical of Judaism, but common throughout much of the Mediterranean world: in Sardinia it became the "spianata"; around the town of Nuoro it was

the "carta da musica" or "sheet music" of the shepherds. The widespread consumption of unleavened bread is demonstrated by many other examples of quite similar methods of preparation, still used in popular recipes in the various regions of Italy. Among the many methods, let me cite only the following: the "piadine," "tigelle," and "burlenghi" of Emilia-Romagna; and the "panigacci" from the area around La Spezia. In the Lunigiana region, these same forms of bread become the "testaroli," a name that derives from the Latin "testum," for the pottery mold in which they were cooked. To take a term from the life sciences, these contemporary unleavened breads are living fossils that tell us much about how bread was produced and consumed in prehistoric times.

It can be determined, in fact, that these thin unleavened breads—aside from being eaten alone, or with cheese or salami, or with vegetable soups—were also eaten with toppings of prepared foods, complete with their own sauces. Sometimes these breads were served with rich sauces that made the dish into a complete meal—not unlike the "panigacci" and the "testaroli," which are traditionally used as platforms for a mushroom-based sauce or for the garlic-free pesto of the Lunigiana. The practice of using an edible plate that becomes savory when soaked in a sauce was handed down throughout the Latin world, right up to the late Middle Ages.

Ancient Roman sign for a
bakery, Museo Ostiense,
Ostia Antica

Large Etruscan oven

Bas relief showing a bakery, Museo della Civiltà Romana, Rome

Clay figurine from Rhodes, mid-fifth century BC, British Museum, London

In this role of supporting and carrying other foods, many of these diverse and quite ancient varieties of unleavened bread already contain the basic principle of pizza. Admittedly, there was no leavening, and the seasoning or dressing was added after the bread-base had already been baked, but we see here the notion of an edible whole, comprising a more-or-less complex topping and a crust made with flour and water. Even after baking, this crust was sufficiently thin that it could be folded and eaten without allowing the seasoning to slip or dribble away.

Leavened and unleavened bread

To return to the history of bread's development, I should point out that the earliest flat cakes of the Neolithic era were not destined to remain unleavened. If water-and-flour dough is left for a few hours before it is baked, natural yeasts present in the atmosphere will almost inevitably induce their expansionary effects. If milk or cheese has been added to enrich the dough, the leavening process will be more pronounced and will occur more rapidly. In all likelihood, the earliest leavened breads were looked upon with a somewhat jaundiced eye because they had an unusual aroma, slightly acid and airy. The first few bites would have shown that the loaves were not dangerous; indeed, since they were softer and easier to chew, they were tastier. Bit by bit, humanity learned to control leavening, and, between the third and the second millennia BC, the process of leavening came to be well understood. At first, the only leavened bread was barley-based; spelt could not be leavened since it had to be toasted before grinding. Later, more widespread cultivation of "naked" grains, those without a glume, made it possible to make leavened bread with wheat flour as well. Just for the record, it should be noted that it was the ancient Egyptians, around the second millennium BC, who first began to study and experiment with leavening. They did not venture into this field out of any desire to improve the quality of their breads; rather it was a need to expand their production of beer, which in those days was made by steeping leavened but only partially baked barley cakes in water. By only partially baking these cakes, the fermenting enzymes were preserved. Gradually, leavened bread—tasty but time-consuming to prepare—became a staple food of sedentary peoples, while unleavened bread—quickly prepared and less perishable—continued to be a pillar of the diet of nomadic peoples.

The Rise of Pizza and the Fall of Rome . . .

In ancient Rome, as early as 200 BC, the "pistores"—millers who had also become public

Paintings from the Golini
tomb, Orvieto, second half
of the fourth century BC

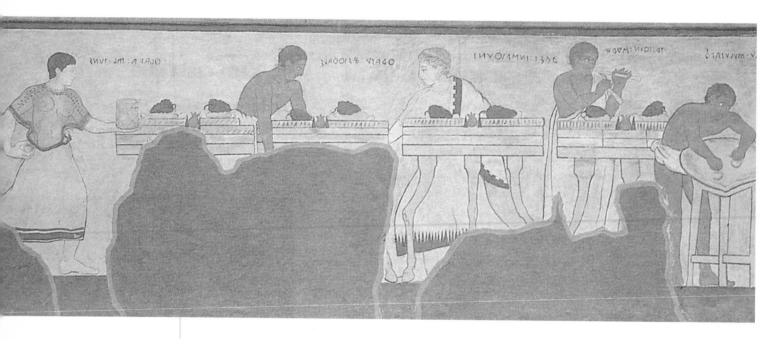

bakers—produced at least fifteen different types of bread, three of which had features that allow us to describe them as ancestors of what we now know as pizza. One of them, called "adipatus," was described as "dressed with lard"—but without any indication of whether that lard was simply an additive in the dough or a topping laid on in slices before baking; if it was the latter, then we could hardly fail to consider this as a forerunner of the modern pizza. The "strepticius," described as a sheet of pastry dough prepared by mixing flour, milk, olive oil, and pepper, and baked on a red-hot slab of stone, may fairly be considered as a full-fledged proto-pizza. Another of these notable baked products, almost certainly of Greek provenance, is especially interesting, because it seems to have been a "pizza bianca," or white pizza, identical, or at least quite similar, to the "pizza bianca" that is still produced in Latium, Tuscany, and Liguria. Its name, in fact—"artolaganum"—seems to have been formed from two Greek words: "artos," leavened bread, though not necessarily made with wheat flour; and "laganon," a thin crust made from a flour-and-water dough.

It is safe to assume that the "pistores" of ancient Rome baked large quantities of "panis adipatus," "panis strepticius," and "panis artolaganum" every day. Still, even though numerous classical authors of ancient Rome—including

Varro Reatinus, Lucius Junius Moderatus Columella, Pliny, and even Cato the Censor—discussed food and cooking, there is absolutely no surviving documentation concerning the consumption of these products. And since they do not appear in *De Re Coquinaria,* the cookbook compiled in the first century AD by Marcus Gavius (known as Apicius), we can assume they were staples in the diet of the plebs, or, in any case, the less well-to-do classes. We must remember that even though *De Re Coquinaria* is a splendid source of interesting information about the culinary culture of Imperial Rome, it contains only the recipes of a wealthy gourmand and ignores the foods eaten by the humbler classes.

. . . and in the Middle Ages

The cultural collapse that followed the breakup of the Roman Empire put a halt to the flourishing literary production that allows us to follow—in however fragmentary a fashion—the development of bread and the accompanying development of baked products that in some way resemble the pizza. We do know, in any case, that during the high Middle Ages there were no more public bakers, and that individual families now prepared and baked their own bread. During this period of invasions and crop failures, it is highly likely that food supplies became unreliable and that the sort of bread-qua-plate became typical of a sustenance diet. It is also likely that during this period some particularly inventive individuals set about modifying the simple "focaccias," or unleavened flatbreads, of ancient tradition, either to enliven a diet made monotonous due to the difficulty of obtaining any but the most basic of foodstuffs, or to make the best possible use of local resources. This would have led to the development of new types of focaccias made with local ingredients. Inexpensive foods like anchovies, sardines, mushrooms, onions, and cheese offered a wider variety of flavors and better forms of nutrition.

These focaccias would, in time, be further perfected. But only with the culinary debut of the tomato before the turn of the nineteenth century did pizza take its next great step forward. Up to that point, we can consider a number of smaller milestones in the history of the pizza. And even though, given their thickness, these were still technically focaccias or flatbreads, not pizzas, they already displayed shared characteristics such as the distribution of the ingredients on the base of leavened dough and the simultaneous baking of the dough and the dressing. The ingredients could be added raw as in the case of the Piscialandrea and the Sardenaira Pizzas developed in the Ponente Ligure. Or they could be pre-cooked, as for the Machetusa, another culinary gem of western Liguria. (The dish consists of a focaccia base with an embellishment of a mushroom gravy, quite similar to the sauce from the Lunigiana that had been used on "panigacci"

and "testaroli" since the days of ancient Rome.)

And there were times when the inspired imagination of folk cuisine managed to come up with full-fledged culinary masterpieces, using ingredients that were as common as they were inexpensive. This was the case, for instance, with the "sfinciuni," a salty recipe of the Palermo region. In this dish the crust is dressed with a rich, nourishing, and tasty sauce in which the clever juxtaposition of the flavors and aromas of anchovies, lemon, and caciocavallo (a strong-flavored cheese from southern Italy) balance the soft, rounded flavor of the dough.

The ingredients may vary, but there is an increasingly clear consensus on what we now think of as pizza. Over the same period, various, almost magical Italian "torte rustiche" (or savory pies) were developed—such as the Torta alle Erbe of the Tuscan-Emilian Apennines; the "Casatiello" of Campania; and the sumptuous Torta Pasqualina and the Torta di Formaggio Marchigiana, both of Liguria. These dishes are distinct from the basic concept of the pizza, but they are significant because they represent a new evolutionary branch in the efforts to ennoble and diversify simple bread.

Evidence of one such effort is a recipe written sometime in the middle of the fourteenth century. It describes the preparation of what we might call a focaccia-pizza; the anonymous

author of that ancient text calls it "migliaciti."
Before being placed in the oven to bake, the
crust of leavened dough, enriched with eggs and
cheese, was covered with a dense creamy sauce
comprising a blend of eggs, cheese, and melted
lard. The "migliaciti" possessed characteristics
typical of both the focaccia and the pizza.

With the exception of this one ancient
recipe, however, there is little written evidence
of pizza or focaccia until the eighteenth century,
even though Italy boasted a rich culinary literature. This literature included manuals of fine
cuisine, written by famous gastronomes for aristocratic tables, but clearly the pizza was considered too lowly a food for serious consideration.

Pizza meets tomato

By the time we reach the seventeenth
century, at least several types of pizza were
common in Naples. Of course these were "pizze
bianche," or white pizzas (because the tomato
had yet to debut), but they were pizzas as we
think of them today. The cheapest version was
dressed with nothing but garlic, lard, and coarse
salt. There was also a richer version, the Mastunicola, which included grated "caciocavallo" and
was seasoned with fresh basil. Since Naples was
a seaside town, we find the first Pizza alla Marinara, or seafood pizza, which featured a sprinkling of tiny fish, known in Campanian dialect as

"cecinielli"; another, richer, version included sunset shells (a variety of clam) and mozzarella.

Still, the gastronomes and chefs of the
time continued stubbornly to ignore the pizza,
considering it too plebeian, too lower-class to
be mentioned even fleetingly in their treatises.
Pizza was entirely overlooked in the treatise *Il
cuoco galante* (*The Gallant Cook*), published in
1773 by the Neapolitan Vincenzo Corrado, who
supervised the kitchen of Don Michele Imperiali,
prince of Moltena and Francavilla. This treatise is
a valuable work because it tells us that by 1773,
the tomato had already entered the cuisine of
Campania, if not the cuisine of all Italy. Thus, we
can establish a firm date for a fundamental step
in the history of the evolution of the pizza.

During the same period we begin to find
the occasional mention of pizza—even though
such references are more on the order of anec-
dotal curiosities. And so we know the story of
Ferdinand I of Bourbon, who loved the simple
foods of his people. He wanted to taste the pizzas prepared in the shop of Antonio Testa (who
was known as "n'Tuono"). The sampling must
have met with Ferdinand's royal approval, since
he attempted to have pizza inscribed in the list
of official court dishes. He was unable to do so,
however, in the face of opposition from his wife,
the strong-willed Maria Carolina of Austria. (It
would also appear that following the royal visit,

Antonio n'Tuono raised the price of his pizza to an astonishing two cents apiece.) Evidently, the love of pizza was hereditary among the Bourbons of Naples, because Ferdinand II, who may have been even fonder than his father of the tasty local Neapolitan cuisine, ordered Domenico Testa—son of the renowned Antonio Testa—to build him a pizza oven in the park of his royal palace at Capodimonte, near Naples.

Pizza triumphs in Naples

Pizza would become one of the most important dishes of Neapolitan cooking by the end of the eighteenth century. Around 1850 it even surpassed in popularity "vermicelli al pomodoro," or noodles with tomato sauce. To understand the pizza's increasing popularity we must consider the social and economic situation of Naples and the rest of southern Italy in the years from the beginning of the eighteenth to the end of the nineteenth century.

The urban poor—sadly, a considerable segment of the population—lived on what they could earn doing piecework and odd jobs, without firmly set hours or a fixed workplace. They would purchase their meals from the numerous local vendors of cooked foods. These vendors thus had a potentially enormous clientele, but to keep that clientele they had to provide nutritious and flavorful foods that could be eaten quickly—since meal breaks were astonishingly brief—and, above all, which didn't cost much.

The "pizze fritte," or fried pizzas, seemed to have popular appeal. These were pieces of leavened dough fried in olive oil. At first they seemed an inexpensive choice, but that soon proved otherwise. The problem was the oil—it had to be kept boiling for hours and hours, and therefore demanded frequent topping off. Moreover, even though there were hardly any health and hygiene regulations to speak of at the time, it was still necessary to change the oil on occasion, or else the "pizze fritte" would be inedible. Unfortunately, olive oil—even bad olive oil—was not cheap, and in time the cost of topping off and replacing the olive oil drove up the price.

Pasta presented a better solution—especially once the tomato made it possible to flavor it with cheap and savory sauces. But pasta was not without its own problems. For starters, it became necessary to meet the demands of the diners who, however poor they may have been, expected the pasta to be cooked *al dente*, as tradition required. A failure to satisfy such expectations might mean losing one's customers. Preparing a series of dishes of pasta properly, *al dente*, with limited utensils, was not an easy thing. Then, once drained and topped with sauce, the pasta had to be transferred into individual dishes or bowls, which involved an

Director Vittorio De Sica in his 1954 film, *The Gold of Naples*

ongoing investment since they would break or simply "walk out the door." Of course, those dishes had to be washed. The labor involved was not itself a problem: any of the starving children who thronged the alleys of the city would gladly do the work in exchange for a portion of vermicelli or macaroni. The problem was that washing plates required the availability of a certain amount of water, and in southern Italy of bygone centuries, water was an expensive proposition. And there was another, even more serious, problem. The traditional depiction of Pulcinella, a greedy buffoon in commedia dell'arte, shows him dangling long strands of spaghetti into his mouth from his upraised hand; in practice, however, using your hands to eat piping hot pasta that is slippery with sauce is hardly inviting. For the urban poor trying to do this in a crowded alley, there was a real danger of someone knocking a precious handful of hot vermicelli to the ground or into one's face. Ideally, each diner needed to be supplied with a fork (let alone a table). But since the fork with four short tines (the one particularly suited for spaghetti and vermicelli with sauce) was not introduced until the middle of the nineteenth century, the serving of pasta as a fast food remained a problem. And when the pasta fork finally made its appearance on the culinary stage (thanks to the Neapolitan connoisseur

Spadaccini), it meant a further increase in costs and a more complicated job of washing for the restaurateur.

Pizza was a perfect solution to the needs of modest restaurateurs and their frugal customers. The only sizable investment was the oven, which really only required some space and some bricks. (If the shop served also as a residence, as was often the case, the oven could be used for domestic cooking and for heating the home during the short but harsh Neapolitan winters.) And folded over on itself as pizza traditionally is, it presents a dry outer surface that is not blistering to the fingers, while the interior remains nice and hot for quite some time. With its thin crust and raised outer lip, a pizza could be held in the hand and enjoyed at leisure, without fear of a jogged elbow spilling one's meal to the ground. No dishes, no utensils, no costly washing up. The restaurateur could offer a relatively broad array of flavors at very affordable prices.

But pizzas couldn't quite get the upper hand over pasta. Even though they were cheaper and more convenient to eat, the traditional "pizze bianche," or white pizzas, were unable to withstand competition from pasta, which was more savory and offered more varied flavors.

It was at this point that some pizza chef (who, sadly, remains anonymous), perhaps in response to the ruthless competition of a nearby pasta restaurant, had a stroke of genius. This chef decided to create a pizza version of the macaroni and vermicelli dishes that were made so irresistible by their savory tomato sauces. The chef must have soon discovered that despite the scorching heat of the oven, the tomatoes kept the thin layer of leavened bread pleasantly moist and soft. The surface of the pizza was spread with the same type of sauce used on the pasta— it only needed to be slightly thinner. And certainly the crowning touch was in replacing the grated sharper cheeses used in pasta sauces with a bit of fine nourishing mozzarella to give these new pizzas a charmingly full and rounded flavor. A brilliant solution, which enjoyed immediate success. It was soon imitated by other pizza chefs so that in a very short time the new "red" pizzas became—at least in Naples and the surrounding region of Campania—the most common form of food.

By the first half of the nineteenth century, the tomato had become an obligatory ingredient for the new generation of pizzas. Tomatoes were so successful that in short order the Pizza alla Marinara (tomato, garlic, anchovies, olive oil) and the Pizza alla Mozzarella (tomato, garlic, mozzarella, basil, olive oil) ascended the Olympus of classical pizzas.

In 1889 it was none other than these two

pizzas that shared the honor with the Mastu-nicola (lard, provola or caciocavallo cheese, basil)—one of the few "pizze bianche" that is still popular today—of being served to their majesties King Humbert I of Savoy and his royal consort, Queen Margaret (Margherita). The royal couple was returning to Naples, where they had once resided, and had expressed a desire to dine on pizza. The dinner went down in history, at least the history of pizza, because the queen so enjoyed her Pizza alla Mozzarella that she wrote a note thanking and praising the chef, Raffaele Esposito. The chef returned the kindness in the only way he knew how: he dedicated the Pizza alla Mozzarella to his queen, dubbing it the Pizza Margherita. As befits such fine food, the new royal name was immediately accepted by all the pizza chefs of Italy.

And yet, despite the fact that the pizza had won both popular and royal favor, the culinary experts of the time continued to snub it. For example, pizza was completely overlooked by Ippolito Cavalcanti, duke of Buonvicino and author of a cookbook in pure Neapolitan dialect, *Cucina casarinola co la lengua napolitana* (*Home Cooking in the Neapolitan Language*). In the book, the duke describes macaroni with tomato sauce and other traditional dishes from the local folk cuisine at considerable length, but he makes absolutely no mention of pizza. This oversight,

however, may have been for political reasons. The first edition of the book was published in 1837, that is, after the hated Bourbon kings of the Two Sicilies had publicly expressed their fondness for pizza. In a historical context, this was the dawn of a struggle that eventually led to the unification of Italy in 1870, and a time of anti-Bourbon sentiment.

After Naples, pizza conquers Italy

Oddly enough, in the years that followed, pizza was still being left out of Italian cookbooks—even those that focused on home cooking for the middle classes. Even Pellegrino Artusi, in his renowned cookbook, *La scienza in cucina e l'arte di mangiar bene* (*The Science of Cooking and the Art of Eating Well*), features a recipe entitled "Pizza Napoletana," or Neapolitan Pizza—recipe number 609. But Artusi ignores what most Napolese of the time called Pizza Napoletana and of which he could hardly have been unaware. Instead of a pizza recipe he offers only a slightly altered version of the "pastiera," a spectacular Campanian Easter pastry. Only the cookbook *Cucina vegetariana e naturismo crudo* (*Vegetarian Cooking and Hearty Naturism*), written at the turn of the twentieth century by Enrico Alliata, Duke of Salaparuta, has a recipe for a Pizza Margherita under the name "Schiacciata alla Pizzaiuola" (a flatbread with peeled tomatoes,

Pizza in the alleyways of
Naples

garlic, and oregano). It is slightly modified, but quite recognizable as the original.

During the period from the turn of the century to the outbreak of World War II, pizza began to grow in popularity throughout the country, even though it continued to be overlooked or ignored by Italy's few official culinary arbiters. The first modern pizzerias began to spring up here and there, and pizza slowly shed its original connotation as a food for the poor, though it still preserved a strong identity as southern Italian folk cuisine. It took a long time for pizza to gain acceptance as suitable fare in many sit-down restaurants, in part because in those difficult years the Italians rarely went out to eat. They tended to cook in and eat at home, and when Italians did feel like spending an evening eating pizza, they usually preferred to bring it home wrapped in heavy paper from the nearest pizzeria. Most often, it was young Italians who dined out in pizzerias. Being less bound by tradition, they enjoyed spending a few hours out of the house in an inviting and picturesque setting. Moreover, in central and northern Italy, pizza became a cheerful byword for a fun-filled evening, and is still considered a food to be eaten exclusively at night.

Around the turn of the century, pizza started becoming one of the most popular and widespread foods in the United States. It arrived with the huge waves of Italian immigrants who for the most part were natives of southern Italy. For these immigrants, pizza (and pasta) remained a symbol of the traditions of their homeland, a staple of their everyday diet. In sharp contrast with Italy during the same years, in America pizza was often a part of the noonday meal of immigrant Italian laborers. By virtue of its appetizing appearance and intoxicating aroma, pizza became increasingly popular with their fellow American workers. This triggered a process that, over the course of just a few decades, made pizza (along with pasta) one of the most popular foods in the United States. In fact, the first pizzeria had begun serving customers in New York as early as 1895.

North American cuisine has a unique ability to adopt the traditional dishes of every country on earth, revise them and present them with their original names, but in often unrecognizable forms. Pizza managed to survive this process of assimilation, miraculously nearly intact. The initial problems of obtaining the proper ingredients led to a substitution of oregano for basil, while garlic basically disappeared from the official recipes, out of respect for the culinary preferences of the Anglo-Saxons. The preparation, however, of the "pettola," the basic disk of pizza dough, and its successive baking, remained as orthodox as could be. Of course, there are

Some imaginative pizza
creations

A calzone

A slice of pizza

exceptions, but they are the exceptions that prove the rule. Pizza conquered the United States and Canada without ever losing its basic culinary identity. It has been a peaceful conquest, and it continues thanks to the efforts of pizza chefs and the increasing ease with which the basic ingredients can be obtained.

In Italy, during World War II, the popularity of pizza stagnated for understandable reasons: young people were off fighting, no one felt like having fun, and during the later years of the war there was not even enough flour to make bread. With the return of peace, however, things changed. Italy was as poverty-stricken as it had ever been, but everyone wanted to enjoy a little illusion of prosperity and some of the small pleasures that they had missed for so long. With the end of the wartime terror, people were happy to go out, and affordable restaurants were always packed with diners. This situation was particularly favorable to the pizzerias of Italy, which sprang up everywhere, from small towns and outlying suburbs to the downtown areas of Italy's largest metropolises. The popularity of pizza burgeoned as well through the efforts of pizza chefs who, in the spirit of earlier chefs, began to interpret the classical dishes of Italian cuisine in the form of pizzas. This creative spark led to the creation of new pizzas—a third generation—alongside the pizzas of the classical tradition (wait until

you see my recipe for Pizza with Gorgonzola and Pineapple). Of course, not all of the attempts at innovation were successful, but some excellent pizza recipes did develop, and in just a few years they won a rightful place on the menus of nearly every pizzeria in Italy. An incredible process of expansion continues even now and, after all these years, there is no shortage of inspiration.

Foremost among these developments has been the transformation in Italy of the takeout pizza establishment. At first these takeout pizzas, or "pizze d'asporto," were just large rectangular slabs of focaccia cut into slices at the request of the customers. These "pizzas" had little resemblance to the actual pizzas whose names they bore. Nowadays, in many places these pizzas are the real thing—with a proper thin, round crust. If not always perfect, they are perfectly acceptable. Though the initial success of takeout pizzas probably came at the expense of genuine pizzerias, today even pizzerias are happy to serve pizza to go, since it lets them increase their sales without increasing the size of their dining rooms. They'll even deliver it— an American innovation that took decades to reach Italy.

The rapid growth of the popularity of takeout pizza could hardly fail to arouse the interest of the pre-packaged food industry. For years the shelves of grocery stores offered

inviting packages that contained uncooked pizza ingredients in perfect pre-measured quantities. By following fairly detailed directions printed on the back of the box, it was theoretically possible to prepare a classic pizza at home. I say theoretically, because despite the acceptable ingredients, the proper pre-measured quantities, and the accuracy of the directions, it was virtually impossible to obtain the promised results because home ovens just couldn't do the job. Recently the food industry solved the problem by offering consumers pizzas that are entirely or partially pre-cooked, then frozen or vacuum-packed; you simply heat them up, in a conventional or a microwave oven. Some supermarkets now offer pizzas prepared on the spot: the

partially pre-cooked crusts of leavened dough are completed with fresh ingredients, and are ready to eat after baking in the oven just long enough for the toppings to cook.

After Italy and America—the world!

Pizza, as we have seen, spread with astonishing speed throughout Italy and the United States. What about the rest of the world?

Except for the United States and Canada, before the end of World War II pizza had not found its place in the daily fare of other nations. In Latin America, the presence of large communities of Italian immigrants led to the creation of a few excellent pizzerias, but problems with the climate and the difficulties in obtaining the proper ingredients hindered the spread of pizza's popularity. In other European countries, the absence of sufficiently large Italian immigrant communities and, especially, the political climate—which worsened in 1936, with the embargo against Italy—kept the pizza well within Italy's borders.

When the war ended, the situation changed radically. Italian emigrants scattered throughout the world, and Italian manufacturers and corporations began to do business everywhere, leading to the constant presence in other lands of Italian engineers and businessmen. But as Americans had seen so many years before,

when Italians travel, their traditional cuisine travels with them—and that includes pizza. And that is how pizza, with its flavors and aromas so reminiscent of bright sunshine, rapidly conquered the taste buds of the world.

RECIPES OF

YESTERDAY AND TODAY 2

66 **If the history of pizza**

can capture our imaginations,

it is no less captivating

to savor pizzas

themselves in all

their infinite variety . . .

RECIPES OF YESTERDAY AND TODAY

There are so many varieties of pizza, and often with so many similarities, that it can be difficult to choose the type of pizza best suited to one's tastes or to a special occasion. But making that choice can also be an extremely pleasant experience.

With a view to assisting the reader who is making pizzas at home or is trying to select one in a pizzeria, I have gathered a considerable number of recipes in this chapter. There are some traditional types of pizza (including more than one historical curiosity), and some more contemporary styles that have been devised to satisfy today's preferences while retaining links to the past.

Let me state clearly that these—or any—pizza recipes should not be considered as carved in stone. Rather, because they form part of an informal culinary tradition, they are often expressions of more-or-less individual dining tastes and habits. And so, even if these recipes are used professionally in most true pizzerias around the world, it may well happen that some pizza chefs, given their creative flair or personal experiences, will eliminate or add this ingredient or that.

However, I strongly advise you not to stray from the preparation and baking of the leavened dough that constitutes the base of all pizzas that deserve the name. If you feel the urge to improvise wildly in your kitchen, I would be the last person to discourage you; but remember, as in any art, great improvisation starts from a great foundation.

BASIC PIZZA DOUGH

Makes 4 crusts (approximately 1 lb/454 g)

2³⁄₄–3¹⁄₂ cups/650–875 mL unbleached flour
1 pkg (or 2¹⁄₂ tsp/12 mL) active dry yeast
1 tbsp/15 mL salt
1 tbsp/15 mL olive oil
2 cups/500 mL lukewarm water
more flour as needed

Sift the flour. In an earthenware bowl, mix the yeast with a little warm water, add a heaping spoonful of flour and blend thoroughly to obtain a dense, smooth, and homogeneous mixture; cover the bowl with a cloth, and let stand in a warm place for half an hour. Pour 2³⁄₄ cups (650 mL) of flour onto a surface dusted with flour, and place the fermented mixture of flour and yeast in the center of that pile. Add the remaining water, the olive oil, and the salt. Cover your hands with flour and knead energetically for about 10 minutes until the dough is smooth and not sticky, adding more flour as necessary—it should not stick to your fingers. Form the dough into a ball, cover it with a kitchen towel, and let it rise for 2 hours in a consistently warm temperature. When that time is up, knead the dough again for about 10 minutes, again with flour-covered hands. Split it into 4 equal parts, and then—using your hands—shape each of those 4 parts into a flat disk roughly ¹⁄₄ inch (¹⁄₂ cm) in thickness, a little thicker along the lip or edge (about ¹⁄₃ inch or 1 cm).

Throughout these recipes I refer to the ball of dough that is tossed to form the crust as the "pettola." "Pettola" means shirt-tail in Neapolitan dialect, and like a fine combed-cotton shirt it must be handled with care. The leavened dough should never be subjected to excessive pressure or, even worse, uneven pressure; otherwise the pettola may take on a rather erratic shape or texture during the baking. For this reason, rolling pins or other mechanical devices are banned during the preparation of the dough. The ideal way to shape the dough into a crust or pettola is to spin it in the air, just the way that professional pizza chefs do it. This is more than mere culinary bravado. The centrifugal force generated by the spinning dough lets you form—without pressure—an almost perfectly round disk of the proper thickness. And if you're careful to leave the pettola a little thicker at the edge, you should even have a raised lip for your crust. If you prefer an even thinner crust than what you get from spinning the dough (it will tear when it becomes too thin), then press down the pettola even more with the hands, working evenly from the center outward on your countertop.

Baking your pizza

Once they have been prepared, dress each pettola according to the recipes you've selected. At that point, the crust changes its status, from pettola to "pizza." The baking should follow specific rules. In a wood-burning oven at 650°F (350°C), baking takes about 4 to 5 minutes. In a normal home oven with the temperature at 450°F (230°C), the time may vary from 15 to 20 minutes, depending on the thickness of the crust.

The best indicator of when a pizza is done is the mozzarella, which is used in nearly all pizzas. When it takes on a handsome glistening color, the pizza is ready. With either type of oven you need to preheat it and maintain a steady temperature.

With a wood-burning oven (after sweeping away any deposits of ash with a whisk-broom), the pizza should be placed directly on the hot surface. With an ordinary home oven, you will have to use a pan or stone that has been preheated with the oven. Only by preheating the pan can you ensure that the bottom of the pizza will stay dry (and won't dry out), while leaving the top and the interior soft and moist. This creates that delightful succession of consistencies that makes every properly baked pizza a small culinary delight.

Ingredients

First, if you're curious about some of the ingredients and possible substitutions, let me direct you to the Notes on the ingredients in the Appendices.

Now, for the preparation of the best pos-

sible pizza, I recommend that you respect the following simple rules. The first has to do with tomatoes. While fresh tomatoes were once all that were available to pizza chefs for making a sauce, they have largely been replaced by canned tomatoes—either in the form of peeled tomatoes or as a purée. There is, of course, no reason not to use fresh tomatoes, but if you do, try to ensure that they are perfectly ripe and stripped of skin and seeds prior to use.

The mozzarella and whatever other cheeses you may be using must be shredded or cut into small pieces, more or less of the same size. This is a fundamental detail because it allows you to distribute the cheese uniformly over the crust. The cheese then melts evenly and lends a consistent thickness to the whole pizza.

While baking in the oven, the crust, sauce, and cheeses are subjected to extremely high temperatures for a relatively short time. So when it comes to raw ingredients (like fresh artichokes or mushrooms), make sure they are cut thin enough that they will cook, but not so thin that they dry out.

Ingredients packed in salt—typically anchovies and capers—should always be thoroughly rinsed, both to reduce the saltiness that would otherwise overpower the other flavors, and to prevent a persistent thirst once you have eaten the pizza. If you use olives, they of course should be pitted.

Since the pettola is made of leavened, salted dough, and since many of the ingredients used in the preparation of various pizzas also contain lots of salt (even if they have been rinsed), it often isn't necessary to add salt to a pizza. Nonetheless, in certain cases it may be necessary to add salt—but always in moderation.

Olive oil, which is the crowning touch on nearly every pizza, should always be applied last. Its main function is to blend and diffuse the aromatic substances contained in the various ingredients. This works best if the oil is poured when all the other ingredients have already been placed on the pettola.

Now, let us move on to the pizza recipes themselves. They are arranged in chronological order, starting with the oldest. Keep in mind that the portions shown for each recipe assume a single pizza, with a ball of dough weighing roughly one-quarter of a pound (130 grams)—that is, one-quarter of the standard dough mixture. A pizza of this size is standard for a one-person meal in Italy. If more than one person is dining, you can make the same type of pizza for each person or a variety of pizzas for everyone to share.

The first "pizza" described is the focaccia, a direct descendant of the sacrificial cakes of the ancient world, followed by a genuine historical novelty—a recipe for what I call the proto-pizza that dates back at least six hundred years.

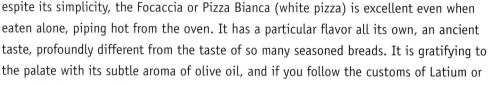

espite its simplicity, the Focaccia or Pizza Bianca (white pizza) is excellent even when eaten alone, piping hot from the oven. It has a particular flavor all its own, an ancient taste, profoundly different from the taste of so many seasoned breads. It is gratifying to the palate with its subtle aroma of olive oil, and if you follow the customs of Latium or Lazio, the taste of the focaccia will be further enlivened by the tiny grains of salt that provide sudden sharp bursts of flavor. The consistency, too—soft yet not puffy, resistant yet not elastic or chewy— makes every bit of pizza bianca a pleasure that involves the entire palate. The thickness of the focaccia makes it possible to stuff it with almost any sort of filling, and in Italy all types of salami are eaten with it. According to the tradition in Latium, the thickness should never be uniform, and the surface of the focaccia should be uneven. In Tuscany and in Liguria, pizza chefs often prefer to make impressions in the surface of the dough using their fingers to do the job. The custom in Latium is to put a tiny bit of salt into the dough, and then scatter the surface of the pizza with large grains of coarse salt. In some areas, they scatter leaves of rosemary or sage on the surface, but that is a matter of taste.

With focaccia alone you can happily drink most any wine at all— be it white or red, including the Spumante Brut—as well as beer, as long as it is not excessively malty (a rule of thumb with pizzas). If the focaccia is stuffed, the stuffing of course will determine what type of wine should accompany it. For example, if it is stuffed with fresh boned sardines, fileted, sautéed, and fried (a remarkable treat), then you will want a fine white wine, not too dry, and a little fruity.

RECIPE FOR FOCACCIA DOUGH

Makes 2 crusts 15 by 10 inch (40 by 25 cm), which would serve up to 12 as an appetizer
pinch granulated sugar
1 pkg (or 2½ tsp/12 mL) active dry yeast
2 tsp/10 mL salt
2 tsp/10 mL granulated sugar
1 cup/250 mL lukewarm milk
6–7 cups/1.5–1.75 L) flour
olive oil
coarse salt
rosemary or sage, a few small leaves (optional)

Warm a large mixing bowl with hot tap water; drain. In warmed bowl, dissolve pinch of sugar in ½ cup (125 mL) lukewarm water. Sprinkle in yeast; let stand 10 minutes or until frothy. To the yeast mixture add the salt, sugar, lukewarm milk, and 1 cup (250 mL) lukewarm water. Stir in flour, 1 cup (250 mL) at a time, until a soft dough forms. On a lightly floured board, knead dough for 5 minutes or until smooth and elastic, adding enough flour to keep it from sticking. Rinse clean the mixing bowl and dry. Swirl a little olive oil over the surface of the bowl. Add dough and turn it over once or twice until it is covered with a thin film of oil. Cover with plastic wrap, then a clean dish towel. Let rise in a warm place for 2 hours or until doubled in

size. At that time, punch it down, replace plastic, and let rise for another hour. Divide dough into 2 equal pieces. Work each into the shape of a rectangle. The dough must be flattened until it reaches a thickness of about ¾ inch (2 cm). Place on prepared baking sheets. Loosely cover with plastic and allow to rise for 45 minutes in a warm place. Preheat oven to 450°F (230°C). Once dough has risen, you can make fairly deep indentations across the surface with your fingers. Brush generously with olive oil, sprinkle with coarse salt and rosemary or sage if you wish, and place in the middle of a preheated oven for about 30 minutes or until crisp and golden brown, tending toward white where the oil has protected the surface from the heat.

Like every proper Roman, I grew up on Pizza Bianca, or white pizza—which in the Latium region around Rome is known as "pizza," pure and simple. It would be served hot for breakfast, and I preferred it greatly to the sweet biscuits of more-typical Italian breakfasts. Another piece of white pizza, this time stuffed with prosciutto, was placed in my book bag, wrapped in waxed paper (no plastic wrap or aluminum foil in those days) for the 10:30 morning snack—or "recreation," as it was known.

In my memory, white

pizza is bound up with summers at Bocca di Magra, where Liguria blends into Tuscany. My family and I would go out sailing on the Leviatano II, a 16-foot pilot boat, and then we would anchor just before Lerici, off one of those broad beaches at the foot of Monte Marcello.

After swimming in crystal-clear water, diving with mask and fins just off the coast (to "build muscles" for the evening's spaghetti dinners), and roasting to a turn in the strong sunshine, we would raise anchor and sail off in search of a cool

haven in the mini-fjord of Maralunga. There we would treat ourselves to a monumental lunch. And even though we wolfed down enormous slices of focaccia stuffed with thick slabs of mortadella, we still managed to appreciate the symphony of delicate flavors.

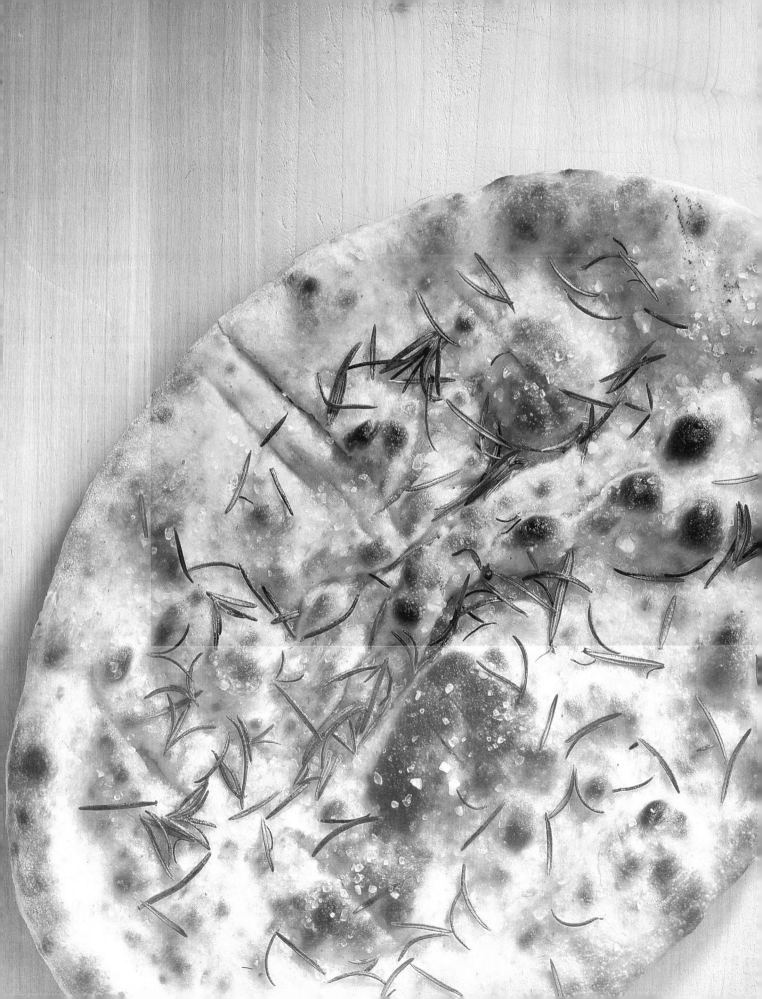

MIGLIACITI BIANCHI E VANTAGIATI (SCHIACCIATE BIANCHE E BUONE)—GOOD WHITE FLATBREADS

ere we have the oldest documented recipe that corresponds to what we call pizza. The original text, in what Dante would call the "vulgar tongue" (the Italian of the period), dates back to the middle of the fourteenth century. The translation reads as follows:

"If you wish to make white flatbreads in the best way that you are able for XII persons, leaven as much flour as will make a loaf and a half, take a little water, nicely warm, and knead the flour well into a dough; then take four fresh cheeses that are nice and fat; and take X eggs and two pounds of fresh lard fat that has been melted over a small fire. And when the flour has been properly kneaded, sprinkle over it a small panful of flour and add a little water, and add three chopped cheeses, and add all the eggs you have, and when this dough is stretched out and soft, place it on the hot (but not too hot) well-greased stone, and grate over it the two cheeses, very fine, and the other half of the lard which you have well heated, and let it cook. And if you want to make it for more persons or fewer, adjust accordingly."

RECIPE

The following recipe is a contemporary variation on the "historic" version above, which used generous, but rather dubious, quantities of a number of ingredients. Makes 12 portions

½ **portion (1 crust) focaccia dough recipe (see page 62)**
5–7 cups/1¼–1¾ L grated **formaggelle (small fresh cheeses made with whole milk) or boconcini (baby mozzarella)**
3–4 eggs
½ cup/125 mL lard or olive oil
flour
water

After the second rising, knead the bread dough with 2–3 cups (500–750 mL) of cheese and a little lukewarm water until you have a fine soft ball of dough. Roll it out and flatten it to a thickness of about ¾ inch (2 cm), sprinkle it with flour, and lay it on a greased baking sheet (as in the focaccia recipe); beat the eggs and blend them with the olive oil (or lard), another 2–3 cups (500–750 mL) of cheese and a little lukewarm water. Spread this mixture uniformly over the dough, then sprinkle it with ¾ cup (150 mL) of cheese. Drizzle with a little more olive oil and bake in a preheated oven at 450°F (230°C) until crisp and golden brown, about 30 minutes.

The culinary structure of this proto-pizza, distant though it is from what we now know as pizza, is certainly nothing to look down at. Admittedly there is little complexity and the recipe does not call for any hot spices, but we do find a succession of soft and gratifying flavors, dominated by the taste of the "formaggelle," or small fresh cheeses. This dish would be best served with a lively and cheerful red wine, not too dry, say a Lambrusco or a Freisa. For those who love white wines, I suggest a Malvasia Secca dei Colli di Parma.

“A recipe for "migliaciti" appears in the *Libro per Cuoco (Book for Cook),* an ancient and anonymous parchment manuscript preserved in a library called the Biblioteca Casanatense in Rome. Linguistic analysis suggests that it was compiled sometime during the fourteenth century by an editor who was born or educated near Venice. Presumably, since it is written in the Italian of the period (and not Latin), the book is a set of instructions intended for the cook of one of the many aristocratic families residing in the region that we now call Venetia. Among the other recipes contained in this little treatise, the recipe for "migliaciti" stands out for its rustic simplicity: there is not a trace of the blends of sweet and savory, none of the abundance of aromatic herbs and spices that—according to the scanty surviving literature from that period—distinguished the cuisine preferred by the nobility and the well-to-do of that age. It would almost seem that a dish from the local folk cuisine had managed to bluff its way into the company of the rich and sophisticated creations that appeared on the aristocratic banqueting tables of the era. Who can say? Perhaps it was a gluttonous caprice on the part of a feudal lord who—like Ferdinand II in Naples five centuries later—did not turn up his nose at the flavorful dishes of the common folk. In any case, "migliaciti" have an importance all their own in the history of pizza because they demonstrate that as early as the fourteenth century a pizza-like dish had already gained widespread acceptance. In a seemingly almost direct line of descent we now have the Pizza Mastunicola. ”

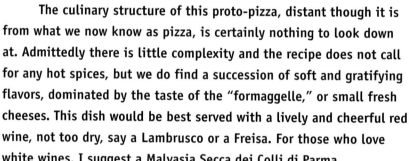

PIZZA ALLA MASTUNICOLA—
MASTER NICHOLAS'S PIZZA

The Pizza alla Mastunicola is an excellent example of fine country cooking. It offers the palate an array of pleasant and satisfying tastes; perhaps a bit aggressive, but honest. The dominant flavor is that of the cheese, enhanced by the soft hints of lard. The prevalent aroma is the fragrant basil that hangs above the sharper smells of the other ingredients. There is also a pleasant counterpoint between the soft consistency of the crust and the more elastic feel of the melted cheese. An attractive array of sensations, in other words, in which all monotony is banished—although, admittedly, the profound flavor of the cheese has a certain tendency to linger on the palate.

RECIPE

1 pettola (see page 58)
4 tsp/20 mL lard or olive oil
¾ cup/150 mL provola or fresh caciocavallo, a strong-flavored cheese from southern Italy (smoked mozzarella or provolone can be substituted)
6 fresh basil leaves

Spread the surface of the pettola with a thin layer of olive oil (or lard). Cut cheese into small cubes and evenly distribute it over the crust. Scatter a few leaves of fresh basil on top, and then bake at 450°F (230°C) for approximately 15 minutes.

Clearly, a pizza of this quality cries out for certain full-bodied reds, such as a Cirò or a Rosso Piceno, or else a white wine with a taste that is perfumed, perhaps with a slightly bitter aftertaste, but not too dry, such as Ortrugo. In short, something that at first sip restores freshness to the palate.

" When we speak of dishes from traditional folk cuisine, it is almost always impossible to establish with accuracy the period in which the recipes were developed. The presence or absence of certain ingredients, however, often helps us come up with an approximate date. In the case of the Pizza alla Mastunicola, we know that it was prepared at least as early as the turn of the seventeenth century, and we can surmise that it dates from a much earlier time. Backing up our hunch, there is a strong affinity between the Pizza alla Mastunicola and "migliaciti," which date back to at least the fourteenth century and were themselves developed as a richer version of an already existing dish from folk cuisine. It seems reasonable to believe that the Pizza alla Mastunicola evolved between the fourteenth and seventeenth centuries, but that its lineage is a good deal more impressive than that.

The exact place of origin of this interesting pizza is unknown, but some have claimed that it arose from the folk cookery of southern Italy in the area we now call Apulia, or Puglia. This hypothesis is based on two pieces of evidence. The first is its resemblance to the oldest known version of the Pizza Pugliese. The second is the name, Pizza alla Mastunicola, which could be a contraction or alteration of the phrase "Pizza di Mastro Nicola," or pizza of Master Nicholas. Nicola is an old and traditional Apulian (or Pugliese) name. There may be historians who disagree with me on this, but as a gourmand I can only say that my logic has the right taste. "

The Pizza alla Pugliese—Apulian-style Pizza—is yet another demonstration of Italian folk cuisine rising to culinary peaks. Here, the entire construction is based on a masterful balance. The flavor and scent of the cheese, robust and sharp, blends with the sweetness of the onion, creating delectable contrasts, underscored by the taste of the crust and enlivened by the scent of the pepper. In an understated manner these contrasts reappear in the consistency of the pizza, which features the sensual yielding softness of the onions and the melted cheese in counterpoint with the chewy resistance of the crust. In short, the Pugliese is a pizza to be admired (and savored) for its many nuances.

Another great virtue of the Pizza alla Pugliese is that it goes comfortably with many different wines—white or red—or even with a good beer. The ideal accompaniment would be a wine, not too dry, with a good but not overwhelming aroma.

RECIPE

1 pettola (see page 58)
¼ cup/50 mL onion
⅓ cup/75 mL aged caciocavallo, a strong-flavored cheese from southern Italy (smoked mozzarella or provolone can be substituted)
2 tsp/10 mL olive oil
black pepper to taste
salt
olive oil

Peel the onion and slice evenly. Sauté over low heat with a little olive oil. Salt very lightly, and distribute onions evenly over the crust. Cover the onions with a generous amount of grated cheese, grind fresh black pepper over it all, sprinkle it with a little olive oil, and put it into the oven at 450°F (230°C) for approximately 15 minutes.

A recent version of this recipe calls for thin slices of blanched potato to be added to the onions. It can be covered with a second crust, and baked for about 25 minutes at 450°F (230°C).

In January of 1948, when I was 18, I ate my first Pizza alla Pugliese in Milan, where I had just moved a few months earlier to attend the university there. The city was entirely foreign to me, and I had begun to systematically explore it. I had been through the entire downtown area, and the time had come to visit the canals south of Milan, known as the Navigli. I decided to venture along the Naviglio Ticinese—a neighborhood that was considered, in those days, rightly or wrongly, the dangerous lair of Milan's underworld. The Navigli fascinated me then as they fascinate me now, but I was disappointed at the overall atmosphere. I had expected a scene out of the movies, but instead I was surrounded by perfectly ordinary people, at least in terms of

appearance: shopkeepers, artisans, factory workers, housewives, and children. It was cold and it was getting to be dinnertime. I decided to go into a small pizzeria in a cross-street of the Corso San Gottardo. Its dirty windows were fogged by steam, and the menu—written on a small chalkboard—featured only three pizzas: Pizza Napoletana, Pizza Margherita, and Pizza alla Pugliese. I had never even heard of the last one. I chose it, partly out of curiosity, and partly because it cost less than the others. As I waited, I wondered whether I had made the right decision—while the restaurant had nothing particularly dark and dangerous about it, it was nonetheless run-down and

dirty. Also, I had not the slightest idea of what I would be served. All doubt vanished as soon as the waiter set the pizza before me. I can still remember my delighted admiration of the thick layer of onions, with their inviting golden-yellow color, against the slightly darker color of the cheese. And then, even more alluring, was the sweet home-cooked smell that sets the Pizza alla Pugliese apart from all other pizzas, a scent that is underscored by the aroma of ground pepper. I greedily ate the pizza with my hands, and wiped my mouth with my handkerchief. In my recollections, that pizza remains one of the best I have ever eaten.

he culinary structure of the Pizza alla Marinara, or Seafood Pizza, is spare and simple. Yet this is a great favorite among serious gourmets and among those who desire nothing more than a tasty pizza to eat with friends. And that should come as no surprise. The overall flavor consists of a dominant note of tomatoes, garlic, and olive oil, melded together by the intense heat of the oven, harmoniously underscored by the homey, gratifying flavor of the crust. The aroma, on the other hand, is the product of a play between the acutely pungent smell of the anchovies and the more persistent, rounded scent of the garlic. These flavors and aromas combine the charm of the sea and the bright hot sunshine reflecting off of it.

Given the presence of the anchovies, it might be best to select a white wine with a lively flavor and perhaps a slight almondy aftertaste that can erase the invasive effect of the garlic. The anchovies make beer a less suitable candidate, but if you do favor it, avoid heavily malted varieties, or what the English term "bitter."

RECIPE

1 pettola (see page 58)
½ cup/125 mL chopped
  tomatoes
2 garlic cloves
4 tsp/20 mL olive oil
2 anchovies

Distribute the tomatoes over the surface of the pizza dough, arrange the anchovies on the surface as well, sprinkle it with the chopped garlic and with olive oil, and then place it in the oven for approximately 15 minutes at 450°F (230°C).

Pizza alla Marinara is one of my favorite kinds of pizza; I have therefore tasted many versions. One Pizza alla Marinara that I remember with particular fondness was baked for me, many years ago, in Carnarvon, a small farming town in Western Australia. I had gone there from Freemantle, where I was covering the America's Cup, to meet the members of a small but flourishing community of Italian immigrants, all originally from the Valtellina, north of Milan, near the Swiss border. My countrymen were farming bananas, mangoes, and other exotic fruit. One evening, my hosts suggested that we end the day with a meal at a local pizzeria. Of course I accepted their invitation, but I must confess that I had some reservations.

The pizzeria itself, they had told me, was not much to look at, but the Aussie who ran it had learned to make pizza in Italy, and,

what is more, had a nice little wine cellar. The pizzeria, at least an hour's drive from the town, consisted of a typical Australian shack made of corrugated sheet metal, but the broad lawn that surrounded it was dotted with long wooden tables with benches. In the middle of the lawn stood an enormous brick oven alongside of which stood an even larger woodpile. The owner and pizza chef, as I later learned, had discovered Italian pizza during a holiday in Italy, and had fallen in love with the food and had decided to open his own pizzeria in Australia. He went back to Italy for a lengthy apprenticeship and, once he had learned all the secrets of the trade, returned to Australia where he opened that odd little pizzeria out

in the far bush. And it was this very man who suggested I order a Pizza alla Marinara, since he did not feel that he could guarantee the quality of the mozzarella that his other pizzas required. He did feel quite confident, though, about the oregano he had grown himself. It was a joy to watch him work against the dark background of the oven, illuminated only by the reddish-yellow gleams of a crackling wood fire.

And a joy—to the taste buds as well as the eyes— was the enormous, perfect Pizza alla Marinara that he then set down before me. To go with it, he served a remarkable Australian Sauvignon—a wine every bit as good as those I knew from Europe.

The Pizza Napoletana, or the Neapolitan-style Pizza, is tasty and stimulating, but also cheerful with its luminous, sunny colors and the dark stripes of anchovies, highlighted by the blackened patches of the charred crust's edges. With every bite the palate is swept by an unexpected harmony of flavors and aromas, alternating and blending as if by magic. Laid over the soft flavor of the crust are the rotund and gratifying tastes of the mozzarella and the tomatoes, sharpened by the bite of anchovies. The initial hint of yeast in the crust is immediately joined by the unusual, slightly exotic scent of the oregano, which in turn gently gives way to the more customary aroma of garlic. All of which is accompanied by an array of alluring, shifting consistencies, soft and yielding but also chewy, yet not excessively elastic, tempered by occasional, surprisingly crisp variations. A concert of smells and tastes that are best enjoyed when the Pizza Napoletana is eaten in the traditional manner: cut up into quarters, folded, and—held carefully with both hands—bitten into ravenously.

The presence of the anchovies demands a white wine, not too dry, better if somewhat fruity and, if possible, with an intense and persistent perfume. No red wines, then, but perhaps a good beer, low on malt, worthy of the flavors and scents of a Pizza Napoletana.

RECIPE

1 pettola (see page 58)
¼ cup/50 mL sliced tomatoes
⅓ cup/75 mL mozzarella
2 anchovies
4 tsp/20 mL olive oil
oregano
1 garlic clove (optional)

Arrange the tomatoes on the pettola. Cut cheese into small cubes and distribute on crust, then sprinkle with oregano, to taste. Cut the anchovies into small slices, and lay them out in a radial arrangement, dividing the pizza into sections.

If you wish, add some chopped garlic. Spread it evenly across the entire surface of the pizza. Finally, dress it with olive oil, and put it into an oven at 450°F (230°C) for approximately 15 minutes.

I tasted my first Pizza Napoletana in 1941, during the Second World War. My brother, who was home on leave from the front, had decided to spend an evening with his friends in a pizzeria just a stone's throw from our home. Though I was only eleven years old, I was permitted to go out with the "adults" since it was a special occasion. I still remember perfectly—this was my first such experience—walking down the short flight of steps into a dark sub-basement, which appeared enormous to my childish eyes. I can also still remember the impressive sight of the stout whitewashed pillars rising up into arches, supporting the dark vaulted ceiling, and the long tables covered with splendid red-and-white checked tablecloths. Then came my first pizza: I tasted it happily, even though I was not quite sure how to eat it. The "adults" ate with their hands, as if it were perfectly natural, even though such a thing was strictly forbidden at my house. I decided to do as they were doing—and it was the right decision.

Thus I began to eat that unknown food with the greed of a hungry child. The anchovies pricked at my tongue and palate, but the combined flavors of mozzarella and tomatoes more than made up for the sharp taste of the little fish, which was itself not entirely unwelcome. At the end of the meal, a splash of white wine was unexpectedly poured into my glass from one of the large carafes. I drank it. Truly it was a night of great firsts.

PISCIALANDREA AND SARDENAIRA PIZZAS— ANCHOVY AND SARDINE PIZZAS

hile there are some great affinities between these two pizzas and the Napoletana, the Piscialandrea and Sardenaira are more starters or snacks than they are meals. Because of the absence of mozzarella in these recipes, the tomatoes and the olive oil can do no more than act as a background for the dominant—at times overwhelming—flavor of the anchovies in the Piscialandrea, or sardines in the Sardenaira. The salted fish offer robust, almost rough sensations, which call for moderation when portioning out the ingredients, even though the soft consistency of the thick layer of dough has a pleasant moderating effect. With their strident scents and flavors these two pizzas have the priceless quality of never—absolutely never—being boring. Every bite offers the palate powerful and nuanced sensations, with a varied and pleasing overall effect. Perhaps, because of the strong taste and pungent aroma that characterize them, Piscialandrea and Sardenaira are not appropriate for an entire meal, but remain—as the people who invented them put it—two unrivaled "spezzafame," or "hunger-busters."

RECIPE

½ **portion (1 crust) focaccia dough recipe (see page 62)**
¾ **cup/150 mL sliced tomatoes**
4 or 5 anchovies
2 tbsp/30 mL olive oil

Roll out the dough with your hands until it is roughly 1 inch (3 cm) thick, lay it out in a pan, and then, pressing on it with your fingers, create small depressions across the entire surface. Distribute slices of tomato across it, lay out the anchovies in a radial pattern, sprinkle with olive oil, and then put it into a hot oven. Given the greater thickness of the dough, it will take a longer time to bake; in a home oven it will take about 15 minutes at 450°F (230°C). The pizza is ready when the surface takes on a nice warm golden color.

If, in season, you replace the anchovies with freshly cleaned and boned sardines, the Piscialandrea is transformed into the Sardenaira.

The Piscialandrea and the Sardenaira are usually cut into small slices and served as a finger food.

Associating a Piscialandrea or a Sardenaira with a white wine is almost automatic—but, I should caution, don't choose any white wine. To best enjoy these pizzas, select a fruity white wine that is not too dry. If you want to follow the traditions of the Ponente Ligure (western Liguria), try a Rossese. A surprising combination perhaps, but this red holds up well to the strongly flavored pizzas.

"I must confess that the first time that I tasted a Piscialandrea, I did so with a certain reluctance, the result of foolish prejudice. While wandering through the Ponente Ligure, or western part of Liguria, I had noticed in the display windows of shops and the counters of bakeries what I took at first sight to be nothing more than a clumsy local imitation of the Pizza Napoletana. Then, one evening in San Remo, I went with some friends from the area to a little local restaurant—the kind with old-fashioned iron tables with marble tops. There wasn't much of a selection: either Piscialandrea or Sardenaira and, to go with them, either red wine (cool from the cellar in stout little earthenware jars) or tap water. I ordered wine and decided to try both types of pizza. I was pleasantly surprised. I discovered that what I assumed was an unimportant local wine was actually a Rossese worthy of the greatest respect, and that the two pizzas, with their strong flavors of the sea, were noteworthy creations all their own, quite different from so many other traditional or innovative pizzas. I also discovered that—flying in the face of the classical prescriptions concerning which wines go with which foods—a red Rossese goes perfectly with the taste and aroma of these two Ligurian specialties. That same evening, my friends explained to me that the name Piscialandrea is a phonetic transcription of the pronunciation, in Ligurian dialect, of "Pizza all'Andrea," because it was a great favorite of Andrea Doria, the great admiral and condottiere (professional soldier) born in nearby Oneglia. Grateful for the lovely evening and the wonderful food and drink, I swallowed this tale too, but I later considered how improbable it was since Andrea Doria died in 1560—long before the tomato had won itself a place in Italian cooking."

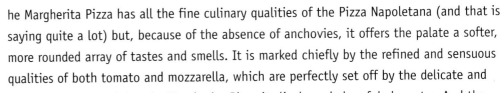

The Margherita Pizza has all the fine culinary qualities of the Pizza Napoletana (and that is saying quite a lot) but, because of the absence of anchovies, it offers the palate a softer, more rounded array of tastes and smells. It is marked chiefly by the refined and sensuous qualities of both tomato and mozzarella, which are perfectly set off by the delicate and distinct undertone of garlic—giving the Margherita Pizza its lively and cheerful character. And the scent of fresh basil banishes any possibility of monotony. But add the basil only after the pizza is partly baked, since the oven's heat can easily burn it or dry it out. The Margherita is a great pizza, particularly appropriate for anyone who is not a fan of anchovies.

RECIPE

1 pettola (see page 58)
¼ cup/50 mL sliced tomatoes
⅓ cup/75 mL sliced mozzarella
1 tbsp/15 mL olive oil
salt
1 or more garlic cloves
 (optional)
basil leaves (optional)

Distribute evenly over the surface of the pettola the slices of tomato and mozzarella. Salt to taste— but not too much—and, if you have decided to use garlic, cut each peeled clove into four or five pieces, arranging them especially near the slices of tomato.

Sprinkle with olive oil, and place in a preheated 450°F (230°C) oven to bake for approximately 15 minutes. If you wish to add a few leaves of basil, do so midway through the baking.

The culinary structure of the Margherita Pizza is nicely suited to many wines; the chief problem is selecting one. In practical terms, nearly any white wine that is not too dry and almost any young and lively red wine—all the better if it is semi-sparkling—would be an ideal accompaniment for this wonderful pizza. For a special evening, you may even give in to the temptation of eating a Margherita Pizza with a Spumante Brut.

" Humbert I of Savoy, as crown prince of the newly united Italy, resided with his consort Margherita in Naples from 1868 to 1871, apparently developing a taste for pizza during those years. When the royal couple returned to the city in 1889 following Humbert's coronation, it seems they requested a meal of pizzas from Raffaele Esposito, owner of the Pietro il Pizzaiolo restaurant in the Salita di Sant'Anna di Palazzo, a narrow cross-street of the Via Chiaia. Raffaele and his wife Rosina must have leapt at the chance of becoming purveyors to the royal court, and so they served up the three pizzas then most widely favored: the Pizza alla Mastunicola, the Pizza alla Marinara, and the Pizza alla Mozzarella (the last of which appeared as early as 1850). Legend has it that Donna Rosina, in a sudden burst of patriotism, bedecked a Pizza alla Mozzarella with a few bright-green basil leaves, so that the pizza bore the three colors of the Italian flag. In any event, Queen Margherita was especially pleased with the Pizza alla Mozzarella, and she expressed her satisfaction in a brief complimentary letter to Don Raffaele. In recognition of the queen's kindness, Raffaele decided to dedicate this pizza to his queen, and he renamed it the Margherita Pizza. The new name was immediately adopted by all the pizza-makers of Naples, and it soon spread throughout Italy. "

SCHIACCIATA ALLA PIZZAIUOLA— FLATBREAD IN THE PIZZA-BAKER STYLE

T he Schiacciata alla Pizzaiuola, taken from *Cucina vegetariana e naturismo crudo (Vegetarian Cuisine and Hearty Naturism),* the cookbook developed at the turn of the twentieth century by Enrico Alliata, Duke of Salaparuta, is a masterful Sicilian interpretation of the Pizza Margherita.

The soft and rotund flavor of the mozzarella, which marks the original Margherita recipe, is replaced here by the sharper taste of a blend of cheeses with much more pronounced flavors. The fresh flavor of basil is replaced by the pungent aroma of oregano, underscored by the profound and persistent flavor of garlic. The result is such a marked set of flavors, with such variable scents, that it might actually be a bit harsh were there not a background of the rich, soft flavor of the "pasta frolla"—or short pastry. In contrast to what we may call conventional pizzas, there is also an array of unexpected tactile sensations: in the Schiacciata alla Pizzaiuola, the fragile rigidity of the short pastry crust sets off the pleasantly soft consistency of the melted cheeses. The result? A pleasantly contrasting arrangement of sensations, typical of many of the great dishes in traditional Sicilian cookery.

For an ideal combination, you should try the Schiacciata alla Pizzaiuola with a red wine—not too dry—with a persistent but not excessively intense perfume. That does not put white wines out of the running, as long as they are fresh and lively and, above all, not too dry. In both cases, semi-sparkling wines will do perfectly. Because of the presence of oregano, it is better to avoid beer with this pizza.

THE ORIGINAL RECIPE

"Make a 'pasta frolla,' or short crust, prepared with 2 cups (500 mL) of flour, ¼ pound (130 g) of butter, a pinch of salt, 1 egg, half a glass of water. Roll it out quite thin, lay it in a lightly greased baking pan, and put a layer of grated mozzarella, some scamorza (a smoked cheese from Apulia or Campania), fresh provolone, or other soft cheese atop it.

"Over that, scatter little bits of skinned and seeded tomato, sprinkle it with chopped garlic and oregano, and put it in the oven at 400°F (200°C) for about half an hour."

66 Enrico Alliata, Duke of Salaparuta, was a truly remarkable man. During the course of his life—he was born in 1879 and died in 1946—he not only successfully directed a major winery, but also worked in many other fields. He was a great gourmet, but also a practicing vegetarian; he personally developed 1,030 recipes, all free of any form of meat. Some of those recipes, because of his culinary genius, faithfully reproduce the flavors, the aromas, and even the consistency of meat and game dishes. He collected these recipes in the book *Cucina vegetariana e naturismo crudo (Vegetarian Cuisine and Hearty Naturism),* with its significant subtitle: *Manual of Naturalistic Gastrosophy, with a Collection of 1,030 Formulas Selected from Every Land.* The cookbook also contains a variety of advice on a proper diet, some of it remarkably valid today. As for the reasons that led Enrico Alliata— who most probably had encountered the Pizza Margherita in Naples, where he traveled frequently—to "formulate" his Schiacciata alla Pizzaiuola, we can only conjecture. He may well have wanted to give a more aristocratic form to the original recipe by replacing the leavened dough with a more refined short pastry crust, and, diet conscious as he was, he compensated for his addition of butter to the dough by eliminating the olive oil. It is less easy to find an obvious explanation for the addition of other cheeses to the mozzarella, and for the replacement of basil with oregano. Perhaps these were choices dictated principally by the very innovativeness that has shaped the evolution of the pizza. Or perhaps Enrico simply wanted to make his pizza more suitable for accompaniment by a greater number of Sicily's wonderful wines. 99

This is a Sicilian interpretation—but a folk version—of the Pizza alla Napoletana. The sharp and strident flavor of the capers holds its own against the powerful taste of the anchovies, and the soft base flavor given primarily by the mozzarella is offset by the sweet but tart flavor of the tomatoes. With their slightly bitter flavor, the black olives eliminate the danger of monotony and at the same time diminish any aftertastes. This pizza is an interesting and skillful balancing of flavors that leaves nothing to chance.

Anchovies, capers, and olives clearly demand that the pizza be accompanied by a fruity white wine, not too dry. Try a full-bodied white, typical of much of the wine made in Sicily. For all your efforts it is never possible to rinse completely the salt from the anchovies and the capers, so the Pizza alla Siciliana tends to make you thirsty. If you are concerned about drinking too much alcohol, choose a moderately malty beer instead—but not too bitter.

RECIPE

1 pettola (see page 58)
¼ cup/50 mL chopped
   tomatoes
⅓ cup/75 mL grated mozzarella
4 anchovies
8 to 10 black olives
10 to 12 capers (rinsed)
1 tbsp/15 mL olive oil

Arrange tomatoes and mozzarella on the pettola, followed by the anchovies, in a radial layout, alternating with the olives; distribute the capers more or less evenly. Sprinkle with olive oil, and put it into the oven at 450°F (230°C) for approximately 15 minutes.

In my memory, the Pizza alla Siciliana is bound up with Parga, a small town on the Ionian coast of Greece, where one August a few years ago my wife and I just happened to find ourselves. We were the guests of a remarkable and charming Greek family, who rounded out their modest income by growing tomatoes and cucumbers and renting rooms to tourists. Their home was quite appealing, and for dining and socializing they had a pounded earth terrace shaded by large oak trees. It was equipped with wooden benches, a few chairs, and a huge table. At the far end stood an impressive Ionian clay oven that George, the father of the family, had built with

his own hands. In the evening, after dinner, we would all relax there and chat in a strange blend of Greek and Italian, eating freshly picked cucumbers and tomatoes, and drinking cold wine or beer. Occasionally, if other guests came late to the house, we would all chip in to stoke the oven and cook enormous pans of moussaka. One day George told us that that evening he had a special surprise in store for us. When we arrived, the oven fire was burning hot. It gave off a familiar, certainly Italian, aroma— which I could not place exactly. My curiosity was not satisfied until George, with a smile that stretched from ear to ear, seized an authentic baker's shovel, or

peel, and triumphantly extracted from the piping hot oven a set of splendid and perfect Pizze alla Siciliana. We enjoyed them with a bottle of a Demestika (which was perfect) that I had managed to find in one of the village shops. George, bursting with pride, explained that he was a "pizzarolo"—he meant "pizzaiolo," the Italian word for pizza chef. He tried to explain to me how he had learned to bake pizza, and why he was especially fond of the Pizza alla Siciliana. But I have to confess that I did not really manage to understand much of the last part of his account. Blame it on the Demestika.

A well-made Pizza Quattro Stagioni is a stimulating combination of flavors. Set against the soft customary backdrop of tomatoes and mozzarella, there is a melding play of the delicate taste of the artichokes and the more intense flavor of the mushrooms. The flavors of prosciutto and salami are enhanced by baking, then enlivened by the anchovies and the olives. This is definitely not a boring pizza. The various consistencies are at times deceptively similar (as with the artichokes and the salami), and at other times sharply contrasting (as with the heat-crisped prosciutto and the mozzarella, which becomes soft and chewy as it melts).

Here, too, there is a vast array of white and red wines from which to choose. A white wine that is not too dry, or a young and not very tannic red wine—either is an excellent companion, especially if it is pleasantly lively. The salami and prosciutto also entitle you to accompany this pizza with a beer; but the presence of artichokes should warn against an excessively bitter brew.

RECIPE

1 pettola (see page 58)
¼ cup/50 mL chopped tomatoes
⅓ cup/75 mL grated mozzarella
¼ cup/50 mL mushrooms
¼ cup/50 mL prosciutto, in thin slices roughly 1 inch (2 cm) wide and ¹⁄₁₆ inch (1 mm) thick
¼ cup/50 mL artichokes
¼ cup/50 mL unsmoked salami in slices roughly ¹⁄₁₆ inch (1 mm) thick
2 anchovies
4 tsp/20 mL olive oil

The artichokes should be sliced very thin,* but first carefully remove all of the tough outer leaves and the internal fuzz. They should be boiled until soft but not mushy in slightly salted water. If you like, after you have softened the slices of artichoke by boiling them, you can sauté them briefly in olive oil, with garlic and parsley. Arrange the tomatoes and the mozzarella on the crust, then distribute all the other ingredients evenly, sprinkle with olive oil, and put it into the oven at 450°F (230°C) for approximately 15 minutes.

*You can also use good-quality bottled artichoke hearts, drained and sliced very thin.

"I have eaten a great many Pizze Quattro Stagioni; I have enjoyed far fewer. In fact, I have not been able to finish some of them. The culinary structure of this pizza, in fact, is quite complex, and all it takes is a tiny error in proportions, or the use of inappropriate ingredients or the improper use of the proper ingredients, to compromise the final result. There are, for instance, certain pizza chefs who—trying to reduce dietary fat—use very thin slices of extremely lean prosciutto on the pizza. As a result, the prosciutto becomes rigid, brittle, and almost flavorless. It also takes on an unpleasant whitish tint as the salt within it surfaces. Sadly, the artichokes often suffer a similar fate. This is inevitably the case when the artichokes are pre-cooked in unsalted water, or if they are not fresh. That is why I recommend sautéing the artichokes briefly with garlic and olive oil before baking with the pizza. I should point out that this pizza too should be lightly dappled with olive oil before baking. If you fail to do so, the crust will turn out unpleasantly dry, and, worse still, the flavors of the various ingredients will not mingle successfully.

And why is this pizza called Pizza Quattro Stagioni, or four seasons pizza? The name comes from the ingredients: the artichokes symbolize spring, tomatoes suggest summer, mushrooms are for autumn, and prosciutto and salami represent winter. Try putting some Vivaldi on in the background for this one. "

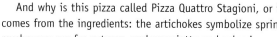

*E*ven though a first glance might suggest that the Pizza Capricciosa is nothing more than a brilliant variant on the Pizza Quattro Stagioni, a closer look soon makes it clear that this pizza is a wholly different culinary construction. What we have here is a constant juxtaposing of tastes, passing, with pleasant continuity, from the soft and rotund flavor of the typical combination of mozzarella and tomato, to the flavor—still rounded, but far more decisive—of the sausage. To liven things up even more, you can add a few capers.

The savory harmony of flavors offered by a Pizza Capricciosa should be complemented by a young and lively red wine that will eliminate the fatty aftertastes of the prosciutto and the sausage. A fruity and aromatic white wine that is, as always, not too dry would make an excellent accompaniment as well—the white also takes into account the sweet aftertaste of the artichokes. An equally amiable companion would be a beer, especially if rich and not too bitter.

RECIPE

1 pettola (see page 58)
¼ cup/50 mL chopped
  tomatoes
⅓ cup/75 mL grated mozzarella
¼ cup/50 mL finely sliced
  mushrooms
¼ cup/50 mL artichokes
¼ cup/50 mL ham sliced into
  lengths
¼ cup/50 mL unsmoked
  sausage or luganega (a type
  of long thin sausage) or
  pepperoni
8 to 10 capers
1 tbsp/15 mL olive oil

Prepare the artichokes as described for the Pizza Quattro Stagioni (page 82); cut the sausage into pieces 3 inch (8 cm) long. (If using round slices of sausage, cut each piece in four, lengthwise.) Arrange the tomatoes and the mozzarella on the disk of dough, distribute the rest of the ingredients, sprinkle with olive oil, and put it into the oven at 450°F (230°C) for approximately 15 minutes.

If you are using unsalted sausage or luganega, you may need to salt the whole pizza to taste.

Pizza Capricciosa for me will always be associated with an unforgettable experience: a wonderful event in human terms, but a culinary disaster. The story dates back to February of 1960, when I was just beginning to discover the joys—and miseries—of everyday life in a small town in the American Midwest. I had been living for several months in a little town of about 20,000 in the heart of Michigan, where everybody boasted ancestors from one European country or another, but almost no one spoke a foreign language—and not one person spoke Italian. I was fortunate enough to strike up a friendship with a delightful couple, Viviane and Don. They were a great help to me in overcoming the inevitable initial prob-

lems of fitting in. And it was Viviane and Don who, when they realized I was very lonesome and blue, organized a "Pizza Party" in my honor. They assured me it would take place in an authentic pizzeria, with a real wood-burning oven.

There actually was a wood-burning oven, but that, unfortunately, was the only resemblance to a genuine Italian pizzeria.

They served us incredibly huge Capricciosa Pizzas—king size, as they put it—that really had very little in common with what an Italian would consider pizza. Suffice it to say that the crust was thick and spongy. I later learned that the dough included milk, and that instead of mozzarella they had used cottage cheese, and that as a substitute for the sausage

they had used a Polish salami that had more garlic than grease (and there was plenty of grease). I could not disappoint my kindhearted hosts and so, with a forced smile, I managed to swallow the monstrous creation that had been set down triumphantly before me. To make things worse, there was a Chianti in flasks that had evidently been terribly mistreated, both in shipping and while it was stored in Michigan. Happily, this improbable Italian dinner was compensated for by the kindness and generosity of my hosts.

I ended up staying an entire year in that town, and I should add that since then I have dined on some magnificent Capricciosa pizzas both in America and back home in Italy.

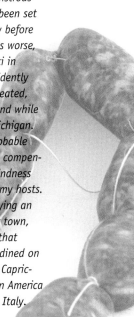

*T*he unquestionable culinary gift of this great little pizza is the balance of the rounded flavor of tomatoes and mozzarella with the pungent, dry taste of the red chili pepper in the salami. The important thing is to create an even contrast. According to some purists, the Pizza alla Diavola should be made without olive oil to preserve the strong aroma of the red chili pepper in the salami slices. On the other hand, the addition of a modest amount of olive oil not only helps to soften the dough, but also spreads a fruity aroma over the entire pizza. Clearly, it is a matter of personal taste.

The presence of the red chili pepper demands (to prevent clashing) that this pizza be eaten with a not-too-dry white wine that has persistent yet delicate perfume, or with a red wine (though not too full-bodied). Not bad with beer at all, as long as the beer is not too malty or bitter.

RECIPE

1 pettola (see page 58)
¼ cup/50 mL chopped tomatoes
⅓ cup/75 mL grated mozzarella
¼ cup/50 mL Salame al Peperoncino (pepperoni) or salami with red chili pepper, stripped of the skin and cut into slices roughly ¹⁄₁₆ inch (1 mm) thick
salt
1 tbsp/15 mL olive oil

Arrange the tomatoes and the cheese on the pettola. Distribute the salami slices evenly over it as well. Salt very moderately and sprinkle, if desired, with a little olive oil just a few minutes before putting the pizza in the oven. This last step will ensure that the spicy aroma of the red chili pepper spreads evenly. Bake at 450°F (230°C) for approximately 15 minutes.

"It is quite easy to make a good Pizza alla Diavola; it is far more difficult to make a perfect one. A great deal depends on the quality of the spicy salami. Too much fat and the pizza will turn greasy when baked; too much red chili pepper and the heat will kill the other flavors and aromas. Also critical is the thickness of the salami slices, and their even distribution over the surface of the pizza. If the slices are too thin, the heat of the oven will scorch them until they take on an unpleasant parchment-like consistency and lose much of their flavor. If the slices are too thick, on the other hand, they will remain uncooked, and therefore quite greasy inside. I remember a skillful Italian pizza chef who opened the first pizzeria in Tarragona, in Catalonia, Spain, at the beginning of the Seventies. He would send to Italy for his mozzarella, but for his Pizza alla Diavola he would use a special variety of "chorizo," the spicy Spanish salami that he had discovered. All of his pizzas were excellent, but his Pizza alla Diavola was nothing short of amazing. With it, we would drink a *vino tinto* (red wine), Vino del Priorato, which in that period could only be bought unbottled, and ranged from 32 to 36 proof. Olé!"

ith this pizza, the palate is pleasantly stimulated by the juxtaposition between the constantly shifting—but basically soft—flavor of the array of cheeses, and the simpler—but still rounded—flavor of the crust. The distinctions between the mozzarella, gorgonzola, Parmesan, and robiola (or similar soft cheese) are subtle but discernible.

It's a harmonious and balanced concert of sensations. If you like, you can have gorgonzola dominate by using the spicy rather than the sweet variety.

The most natural accompaniment is a young and lively red wine, not too full-bodied, never tannic, and if possible, slightly sweet. There are other excellent possibilities, such as white wines that are sweetish or even sweet, with an aromatic bouquet. The ideal selection, however, because of the gorgonzola, is a sweet aromatic, semi-sparkling Moscato dell'Oltrepò Pavese.

RECIPE

1 pettola (see page 58)
⅓ cup/75 mL grated mozzarella
¼ cup/50 mL gorgonzola
(sweet or spicy, as
preferred)
¼ cup/50 mL soft cheese,
such as robiola or stracchino
(smoked mozzarella or provolone can be substituted)
4 tsp/20 mL grated Parmesan

Mix together the mozzarella, the gorgonzola, and the soft cheese, then scatter them evenly over the surface of the disk of dough and sprinkle with Parmesan cheese before placing into the oven.

"I shall likely never learn who invented the Pizza ai Quattro Formaggi, but I owe that chef a debt of undying gratitude because this very pizza has allowed me, and continues to allow me, to cope with an ongoing philosophical dilemma. I have a very dear friend from India, Pradip, with whom I share some common interests. Pradip occasionally comes to Milan on business. Because he is very busy and keeps odd hours, the only time we can manage to get together is for dinner, and this is where the dilemma exists. Pradip is a practicing Hindu and therefore a strict vegetarian. Moreover, he dislikes all pasta—no matter how it is prepared. This makes it pretty difficult for us to find a good dinner for Pradip in Italy. At first I had no idea how to solve the problem, but then I had an illumination: why not try a pizza? After all, it's quite similar to the Indian way of eating chapatis, and it might even soothe some of Pradip's lingering homesickness. The idea was a good one, and it was none other than the Pizza ai Quattro Formaggi that particularly pleased my friend. After a first, hesitant bite, he fell in love with the pizza. Since then, whenever Pradip comes to Milan, we somehow find an evening for us to have dinner. We discuss many things—from the transmigration of souls to the role of women in modern Indian society—while eating a spectacular Pizza ai Quattro Formaggi or two. I should add that my friend's religious beliefs do not forbid him to drink wine; at times, our theosophical and social disquisitions become somewhat muddled."

PIZZA AI FUNGHI PORCINI—PIZZA WITH PORCINI MUSHROOMS

*T*his superb pizza was certainly created by someone with great culinary skills. The chef replaced a béchamel pasta sauce with a nicely balanced blend of mozzarella and grated Parmesan cheese that was capable of surviving the intense heat of baking. The result, in gastronomic terms, is truly exciting.

In this pizza, the prevailing taste is the rich and persistent flavor of mushrooms, which is at once underscored and also, in a sense, mitigated by the rounded flavor of the cheeses. Also, the slightly pungent aroma of the leavened dough balances the mossy and sensual scent of the mushrooms, giving the palate an opportunity to appreciate that aroma at its finest. Excellent on any occasion, and nothing less than perfect for a special evening.

This magnificent pizza has a rich flavor and aroma, and should be accompanied by a young red wine of high quality and not too strong a bouquet. The pizza also goes very well with a good Spumante Brut, which with its delicate aroma will enhance the earthy scent of the mushrooms without clashing with it.

RECIPE

1 pettola (see page 58)
½ cup/125 mL porcini mushrooms*
⅓ cup/75 mL mozzarella
4 tsp/20 mL grated Parmesan cheese
salt
1 tbsp/15 mL olive oil (optional)

Cut the mushrooms into very thin slices and arrange them uniformly over the surface of the disk of dough, along with the mozzarella. Salt moderately, sprinkle with grated Parmesan. If you wish, dribble on some olive oil before putting into the oven. Bake at 450°F (230°C) for approximately 15 minutes.

*Porcini mushrooms are usually only available dried. Soak dried porcini in warm water to cover. Let stand for about 30 minutes. Drain through cheesecloth or fine sieve to eliminate grit. Save liquid for soups, risotto, or sauces.

I had the best Pizza ai Funghi Porcini of my entire life in a small pizzeria in the Lunigiana; a pizza worthy of note because it also managed to save an evening that began quite badly. Some friends, my wife, and I were at Portovenere, around the middle of a September that had begun beautifully but then turned rainy and depressing. And so, one evening, we decided to venture out into the rain and take a little drive to Pontremoli to have a dinner of "testaroli" and "torta rustica," the local specialty. Testaroli is a type of regional pasta, square- or diamond-shaped, dressed with pesto and pecorino cheese; and

torta rustica is a cheese and meat "pie." Since it was no longer the height of the tourist season, we did not bother to call ahead to make a reservation. Apparently half of the Lunigiana region had had the same idea, and in fact all the restaurants were crammed full and booked until closing. It was getting late, and we decided to head home, hoping to find any place along the way where we could stop for a bite. A few miles outside of Aulla we saw a sign for a pizzeria. It was not what we had been hoping for, but we stopped all the same and were lucky enough to get a table. I was about to order my usual Pizza Margherita when I noticed

that the menu also featured Pizza ai Funghi Porcini, and alongside, written by hand, a little note: fresh mushrooms. I was tempted, and soon I was served a pizza that was literally covered with thinly sliced mushrooms with a delicious meaty texture and steaming with an aroma that to me, perhaps because of my hunger, seemed absolutely heavenly. After we had eaten, I wanted to offer the chef my compliments for the perfectly prepared pizza I'd just eaten. He was a young man from the area, and—with laudable modesty—suggested that what had made the pizza so good was probably the very fresh mozzarella.

PIZZA AL PROSCIUTTO E AI FUNGHI—PIZZA WITH HAM AND MUSHROOMS

The Pizza al Prosciutto e ai Funghi is not merely a retooled version of the Pizza ai Funghi Porcini; the basic premise and the culinary structure are, in fact, entirely different. The mushrooms have, this time, only a co-starring role. Their aroma, less intense than that of porcini mushrooms, will meld with that of the tomato and the perfume of the baked ham, creating an alluring fragrance that is gently underscored by the hints of garlic in this complex recipe. Once again, the soft taste of mozzarella and tomato will dominate, followed by the slightly pungent flavors of the mushrooms and the ham. If you like, add a light dusting of freshly ground white pepper to the pizza as soon as it's baked.

RECIPE

1 pettola (see page 58)
¼ cup/50 mL chopped
   tomatoes
⅓ cup/75 mL grated mozzarella
¼ cup/50 mL ham, sliced
   2 inch (5 cm) long and
   ½ inch (1 cm) wide, and
   roughly ¹⁄₁₆ inch (1 mm)
   thick
¼ cup/50 mL mushrooms
1 garlic clove
4 tsp/50 mL olive oil
salt
freshly ground white pepper
   (optional)

Arrange the tomatoes and the mozzarella on the pettola, then evenly distribute the slices of ham, the mushrooms (cut into very small pieces), and the garlic (finely minced). Salt moderately, sprinkle with olive oil, and put pizza into the oven at 450°F (230°C) for approximately 15 minutes. When it is baked, you can dust with freshly ground white pepper.

Despite its fairly complex blend of flavors, this pizza goes quite well with either red or white wines. The reds in this case should be full-bodied with a marked bouquet, while the whites—which should have a perfume that is as persistent as it is intense—will ideally have a bitter or almondy aftertaste. This pizza will also go well with beer that is bitter, but not too malty.

From 1960 until 1975 my family accompanied me as I traveled the world for work. We enjoyed a variety of culinary cultures, but in most of them tomatoes weren't used as a standard base for meat or other sauces. My daughter Donatella, although only four years old at the beginning of our fifteen-year odyssey, developed a remarkable longing for what she called "i sughi rossi," or the red sauces that she had tasted back home in Italy. As a result, she became partial to almost all kinds of pizza with the cheerful hues of tomato. However, it was only during a holiday in Italy toward the end of the 1960s, when Donatella was about twelve, that she first tasted Pizza al Prosciutto e ai Funghi, which my wife had ordered. It was true love at first bite, and the love affair continues to the present day. Thirty years later, the Pizza al Prosciutto e ai Funghi remains her unquestionable favorite.

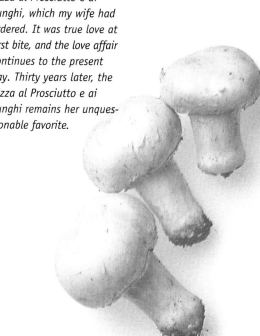

his is a spectacular pizza that balances the bitter aftertaste of grilled eggplants with an appetizing mix of tomatoes, garlic, basil, and olive oil. In short, another small masterpiece of rustic cuisine. The aroma smacks of summer and sunshine and the pizza can be made even better by a slight sprinkling of white pepper, ground fresh.

RECIPE

1 pettola (see page 58)
½ cup/125 mL chopped
  tomatoes
⅓ cup/75 mL grated mozzarella
½ cup/125 mL eggplant
  (about ½ medium-sized
  eggplant), cut into slices
  ⅛ inch (3 mm) thick and
  grilled
6 to 8 capers (rinsed)
1 garlic clove, minced
6 basil leaves
salt
2 tbsp/30 mL olive oil
freshly ground white pepper
  (optional)

On the crust arrange the mozzarella and half the tomatoes. Scatter the minced garlic over it, and evenly distribute the capers, the slices of eggplant, and the basil leaves. Salt moderately, sprinkle with olive oil, scatter the rest of the tomatoes over it, and place it in the oven for approximately 15 minutes at 450°F (230°C). When it is baked, you can dust with freshly ground white pepper.

The Pizza alle Melanzane easily lends itself to both white and red wines. With whites, veer toward a wine with an intense bouquet— better if fruity—and a moderately dry and savory quality followed, if possible, by a sharp almondy or bitterish aftertaste. Reds should have a certain amount of body but not be too dry; the bouquet should be intense and persistent. As for beer, the robust flavor of the Pizza alle Melanzane demands something that is not too bitter and only moderately malty.

66 Pizza alle Melanzane is another example of the successful transfer of a great culinary tradition into a pizza version. Here the original dish is Parmigiana di Melanzane, or Eggplant Parmesan. In the translation, the pizza version required a number of modifications, both in the proportions and the preparation of the ingredients. This pizza requires more olive oil than usual (the eggplant tends to absorb it). It also uses more tomatoes, which are arranged in a double layer to keep the eggplant (which has already been grilled) from drying out or being charred while baking. (Charring can produce an unpleasant consistency or, worse still, an unpleasant bitter taste.) The pizza recipe was developed with an eye to today's more health-conscious tastes. Although the eggplant is no longer fried—as Eggplant Parmesan traditionally requires—but grilled to reduce the amount of fat, the Pizza alle Melanzane remains a classic culinary achievement. But why do I praise this pizza so highly?

First, because it recalls the ancient custom of the "mensae," with its base of leavened dough supporting a richly aromatic meal. Second, because it is truly a tasty dish and one that I invented myself (in the recipe presented in this book, at least). And human vanity, after all, really has no limits. 99

*L*ike the Pizza alle Melanzane, the Pizza alla Pescatora is the result of an Italian folk dish being carried over into the context of pizza. In the original dish, Spaghetti ai Frutti di Mare, the combination of tomatoes with garlic and parsley provides the flavor foundation for the seafood toppings. The pizza version adds one further dimension: the soft, almost earthy consistency of the dough. Normally, Pizza alla Pescatora is made with canned mussels, which are perfectly fine. But here I have chosen to use fresh "frutti di mare," or an array of Italian shellfish. This requires more work and takes more time, but the results are spectacular. The liquid you get from pre-cooking the shellfish is a full-bodied broth that gives the entire pizza a wonderfully distinctive taste. Remember though, you can use canned "frutti di mare," or even just clams or mussels, without diminishing the final outcome. Whatever your selection, the aroma is deeply exquisite. Combine the soft consistency of the base with the delicate tastes and textures of the shellfish and the result is remarkable—a profound harmony of land and sea.

With the Pizza alla Pescatora there can be no doubt, no hesitation: a white wine, with a delicate bouquet so as not to overpower the aroma of the shellfish: a dry or sweetish selection, as you prefer, or even a Spumante Brut will enhance the flavors and textures offered up by this most excellent pizza.

"I still remember with pleasure a Pizza alla Pescatora that I ate in Freeport, Texas, in the home of a family of distant Italian origins—third-generation Americans. They had not forgotten traditions and boasted (alongside their barbecue) a splendid wood-burning oven. For our "frutti di mare" there were only clams—the American equivalent of Italian "vongole"—enormous but incredibly fresh, and even though the parsley wasn't quite up to scratch, the pizzas were truly outstanding. We drank a California Sauvignon with it, and for me, after a week of intense travel and fast-food, it was an evening to remember."

RECIPE

1 pettola (see page 58)
½ cup/125 mL chopped tomatoes
8 mussels, scrubbed and debearded
12 large clams, scrubbed
2 Capasanta, or pilgrim scallops (large scallops, with roe attached if possible), rinsed
1 garlic clove, minced
1 tbsp/15 mL parsley, minced
salt (optional)
1 tbsp/15 mL olive oil

Place scrubbed clams (still in their shells) in a pan—without water—allowing them to open over a moderate heat. Remove clams from their shells and set them aside. (Always throw away shellfish that fail to open.) Filter the liquid yielded by the clams, and set it aside. Place scrubbed mussels (still in their shells) in a steamer with a little water and bring to a boil. When the shells open, remove mussels from pan. Arrange the tomatoes on the crust, sprinkle with garlic and parsley, and moisten with the clam broth. Sprinkle with olive oil, and put the pizza into the oven for approximately 15 minutes at 450°F (230°C). After about 12 minutes, remove from the oven and arrange the shellfish, including the scallops, on the pizza. Put back in the oven for about 3 minutes to finish baking.

PIZZA ALLE ZUCCHINE E GAMBERI—PIZZA WITH ZUCCHINI AND SHRIMP

*A*s you eat this pizza, your taste buds are caressed by a fascinating succession of flavors. The crust is topped by the slightly grassy taste of zucchini, the entrancing mix of the cheeses that have melted during the baking, and finally the tender taste of the shrimp with the tang of the sea. And don't forget the sparks of mint and the burnt taste of the charred bits from the lip of the pizza crust.

Of course, the presence of shrimp dictates a white wine—indeed, a fine white wine, since it will accompany such delicate tastes and aromas. A Vermentino, or perhaps a Cinque Terre, or even—if the occasion calls for it—a Prosecco or—why not?—a Brut.

RECIPE

1 pettola (see page 58)
1 small zucchini, trimmed
6 zucchini blossoms (rather large)
6 shrimps (average size)
4 tsp/20 mL olive oil
nepitella (calamint) or a few leaves of mint and oregano
1 tbsp/15 mL grated Parmesan cheese
1 tbsp/15 mL grated pecorino cheese, moderately aged
salt
white pepper

Cut the zucchini into round slices about ¹⁄₁₆ inch (1 mm) thick, and blanch them for a minute or two in salted boiling water; briefly boil the shrimps in salted water and shell them. On the crust, arrange the blossoms and the sliced rounds of zucchini, radiating out from the center; sprinkle them with the grated cheeses. Add the finely minced calamint, dribble with olive oil, and put the pizza in the oven at 450°F (230°C) for approximately 15 minutes. After about 12 minutes, remove it from the oven, lay the shrimps on it in a starburst pattern, put the pizza back in the oven, and finish baking.

Add freshly ground white pepper before serving.

" I must begin by explaining that, while the Pizza alle Zucchine e Gamberi, or pizza with zucchini and shrimp, is not particularly well known, it does have a precise date of origin: April 1995. How do I know this?

Right across the street from where I live is a small bakery. The baker, Vittorio, forever complains about variations in the quality of the yeast he uses and the fluctuations in his oven temperature. But every day he produces excellent bread and yards and yards of excellent takeout pizza (or perhaps I should say focaccia, given the thickness). The pizzas, for the most part, are traditional varieties, but there are a few variations inspired by the vegetables in season. Among these, the zucchini pizza stands out. My wife and I occasionally rely on Vittorio's pizzas for a tasty but quick lunch. Normally we order our favorites—Pizza Margherita and Pizza alle Cipolle—but sometimes out of curiosity we order one of Vittorio's inventions. And so, some years ago, at the beginning of April, we tried Vittorio's zucchini pizza and—to tell the truth—we weren't crazy about it. The pizza featured little round slices of zucchini laid out on a disk of leavened dough, and then baked in the oven. Despite the fact that the pizzas were generously flavored with grated Parmesan cheese, olive oil, and salt, they didn't taste like much. While we were eating it, we recalled a delicious plate of tagliatelle with zucchini blossoms and shrimp that we had once eaten in Quercianella, just south of Livorno (Leghorn), and it immediately occurred to us to use that recipe to improve Vittorio's Pizza alle Zucchine. I discussed the matter delicately with Vittorio and, after lengthy negotiations, he agreed to attempt the dish on the understanding that I would obtain the ingredients myself and, above all, that the experiment would be conducted at six in the morning, between batches of bread. And so, in those pre-dawn hours, we prepared the first Pizza alle Zucchine e Gamberi in history. It was a great success—so much so that we drank to it, cheerfully finishing off the entire bottle of S'eleme wine that I had brought with me. Vittorio, however, rightly observed that the preparation was time-consuming and his necessarily higher price would discourage most of his regular customers from ordering it. A pity, because this is truly a notable pizza. I offer it now in the hope that it will find a place on the menu of some enterprising pizza chef out there. "

he quality of the Pizza al Tonno is the result of a balancing of flavors and perfumes. The most difficult challenge comes from the anchovy; if you use too much it could dominate, overwhelming all the other flavors. For that reason, I suggest sticking to the recommended amounts. Do so and you'll find that the final result is truly amazing—especially if you liven things up by adding some red chili pepper just as the pizza is being served.

As I've already pointed out, the presence of anchovy, even in small quantities, demands a certain caution in the choice of wine. A white wine, of course, but not too dry—best, in fact, if sweetish: fruity and with a good, persistent aroma. The Pizza al Tonno can also be enjoyed quite nicely with a beer, but not too bitter, or it will clash with the anchovy.

RECIPE

1 pettola (see page 58)
¼ cup/50 mL chopped
   tomatoes
½ anchovy
¼ cup/50 mL canned tuna
1 garlic clove
6 to 8 capers
1 small bunch parsley, stems
   trimmed
4 tsp/20 mL olive oil
red chili pepper, powdered
   (optional)

Mince together the anchovy, capers, garlic, and parsley. Drain the tuna thoroughly and break it into large chunks. Place the tomatoes on the crust, arrange the minced ingredients and the chunks of tuna evenly over the crust, sprinkle it with olive oil, and put it into the oven for approximately 15 minutes at 450°F (230°C). If you wish, sprinkle on a little red chili powder just before serving the pizza.

In my mind, Pizza al Tonno is forever linked to a warm June evening three or four years ago, and a small pizzeria somewhere between Amalfi and Salerno. The weather was beautiful, and, while I was not particularly hungry, I did want to enjoy the spectacular sunset, sitting in a cool spot and sipping a few glasses of properly chilled white wine. I was with my family and we spotted a ramshackle pizzeria, set a short distance from the road. In the back, protected from the bustle of the passing traffic, there was a little pergola with a few tables, each set with the familiar checkered tablecloth. We sat down and ordered a house wine, which turned out to be a genuine Greco di Tufo, and we began to read the menu. My eye fell on the Pizza al Tonno, which I had never tried before. I ordered it, somehow certain that it was made with fresh tuna. When the pizza arrived and I saw that it was made with canned tuna, I was a little put out. But my mood improved as soon as I swallowed the first few bites. I finished the pizza, polished off the last few drops of wine, and went to pay my compliments to the chef— and to ask if he would reveal the secrets of his fantastic pizza. And as we enjoyed a glass of chilled Limoncello (a lemon liqueur) together, he explained to me in his colorful dialect the various steps involved right down to his wife's careful mashing of capers, anchovies, parsley, and garlic. There was just one detail on which we did not entirely agree: whether a little red chili pepper should be added to the baked pizza. To his mind, it harmed the pizza's flavor; I am still convinced that it goes perfectly.

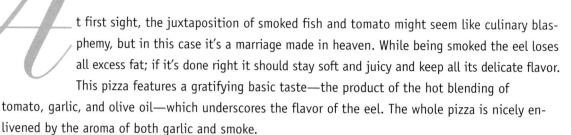

t first sight, the juxtaposition of smoked fish and tomato might seem like culinary blasphemy, but in this case it's a marriage made in heaven. While being smoked the eel loses all excess fat; if it's done right it should stay soft and juicy and keep all its delicate flavor. This pizza features a gratifying basic taste—the product of the hot blending of tomato, garlic, and olive oil—which underscores the flavor of the eel. The whole pizza is nicely enlivened by the aroma of both garlic and smoke.

A white wine, certainly, but not too sweetish, and, if possible, with a slightly acid and fruity foundation, to eliminate the slightly oily aftertaste of the eel. The pizza is also good with beers that are not too malty, especially if they are moderately bitter.

RECIPE

1 pettola (see page 58)
½ cup/125 mL chopped tomatoes
3 oz/80g smoked eel (or other smoked fish, such as haddock or cod)
½ garlic clove
salt
1 tbsp/15 mL olive oil

If eel is difficult to find, use any kind of smoked fish. Make sure all the bones are removed. Cut it into 1 inch (3 cm) squares. Mince the garlic very fine. Arrange the tomatoes on the crust, salt to taste, and scatter the minced garlic on top. Evenly distribute the squares of fish, sprinkle with olive oil, and put it into the oven for approximately 15 minutes at 450°F (230°C).

I had long heard of the existence of Pizza all'Anguilla, but I had never managed to find a pizzeria that served it, and so—deceived by my memories of sumptuous Danish and Swedish "smørrebrød" in which smoked eel plays a prominent role—I was beginning to think that it was a pizza made only in Scandinavia. But I finally happened on it in a pizzeria on the east coast of Italy in the Marche region, just outside of Porto San Giorgio. It was still early spring, rainy and cold, that sad period when most of the seaside restaurants are still closed. I was in an area that I did not know very well, and since it was late I didn't feel like searching for a restaurant or a trattoria willing to feed me. I spotted a pizzeria blazing with a neon sign that told me the place was still open, and that it featured a wood-burning oven. The interior was cozier than the outside might have suggested, and the oven was brimming with activity under the watchful eyes of two pizza chefs. On the menu, alongside most of the traditional pizzas, was the very Pizza all'Anguilla that I had wanted to taste for so long. I ordered it, not quite sure what I was going to get, but my misgivings vanished as soon as the pizza was served. The aroma was good and the taste was even better. I drank a Verdicchio di Matelica—suggested by the waiter, who really knew his wines. The wine had a pleasant aftertaste of green apple: a perfect complement to this delightful pizza.

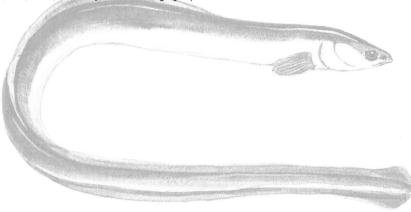

*A*t first blush, one might think that the makings of the Pizza alla Tedesca are really, all things considered, rather obvious. But that is not the case. Note, for instance, the choice of smoked provola, which eases the transition from the sweet aroma of the yeast in the crust to the more pungent smells of the frankfurters and the speck. It's an interesting combination because of the succession of soft and rounded flavors, a sequence that might become tedious were it not for the gherkins that perkily eliminate any aftertaste. A slightly unusual pizza, admittedly, but not without its charms.

Created to satisfy northern tastes, this pizza goes perfectly with beer, especially if it is light and not too malty. Pizza alla Tedesca also goes nicely with wine, either red or white, as long as it is not too full-bodied. In other words, a young wine, preferably with a slightly bitter or acid aftertaste, which will go well with the gherkins.

RECIPE

1 pettola (see page 58)
1 medium onion
¼ cup/50 mL smoked provola or provolone cheese
3 frankfurters (average size) or good quality German wurst
6 slices of speck or smoked bacon
2 tbsp/30 mL gherkin pickles, coarsely chopped
salt

Peel the onion, cut it into thin slices, let it stand briefly in salted water, and then drain it thoroughly. Cut the frankfurters in half, lengthwise. Distribute the cheese on the crust evenly, alternating with the frankfurter and speck slices. Scatter the sliced pickles over the top, and place the pizza into the oven for approximately 15 minutes at 450°F (230°C).

Toward the end of the Sixties, I traveled all over Germany, wandering for weeks at a time, almost always in the company of my friend Knud, a likable former champion oarsman who is plagued by insatiable hunger. Every time I visit Knud's home in Düsseldorf, we spend a pleasant evening or two together. Typically, we end up in the grip of nostalgia and go to one of the few surviving taverns that serve only roast chicken and fried potatoes—places where, thirty years ago, Knud could spend just a few marks and feast like a wolf, eating two whole chickens heaped with mountains of potatoes. On one of my most recent trips, however, my friend insisted that we go to a pizzeria run by Italians—who were, in fact, Spaniards. Predictably, the pizzas were huge. And though they were properly baked in a wood-burning oven, they looked kind of odd to me.

I was curious, however, and so I followed Knud's example—he was familiar with the place—and ordered the Pizza alla Tedesca, or German-style pizza, which I had never tasted before. I was more than satisfied, and despite its size I finished my pizza quickly. A couple of bottles of a young and cheerful Rhine wine, with a light and pleasantly bitter taste, helped move the meal along.

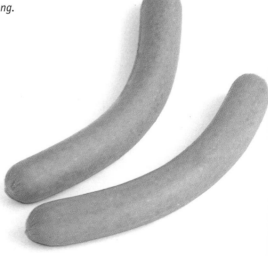

Clearly, this is an American interpretation of the Italian concept of pizza but, all things considered, it is pretty close to the mark. There is a pleasant succession of mild and savory tastes, enlivened by the pungent aroma of the oregano, which also cuts through the aftertastes of the peppers and sausage. It's a pizza that in all essentials mirrors the classics of Italian pizza.

Pizza with Sausages does not feature flavors or aromas that clash with any wines or beers. So you can choose freely among red or white wines, or any of the lighter lagers or ales you wish.

RECIPE

1 pettola (see page 58) about 24 inch (60 cm) across (double dough recipe if necessary)
1 cup/250 mL tomato sauce (recipe follows)
1 cup/250 mL grated mozzarella
1½ cup/375 mL red or green peppers, thinly sliced
½ lb/250 g sausage, cooked and sliced
1 tbsp/15 mL oregano
1 tbsp/15 mL olive oil

Spread the sauce over the crust, and distribute the mozzarella, the thin slices of pepper, and the sausage. Sprinkle with oregano, and then with oil, and put into the oven for 15 to 20 minutes at 450°F (230°C).

Tomato Sauce
¼ cup/50 mL tomato purée
olive oil
¾ cup/150 mL tomatoes, peeled
1 small carrot, grated
black pepper
4 tsp/20 mL butter
dried basil

Make the tomato sauce by sautéing the tomato purée in a little olive oil, then add the peeled tomatoes, the grated carrot, a pinch of black pepper, the butter, and the dried basil. Simmer for 45 minutes.

66 The popularity of pizza in the United States is truly amazing. In just over one hundred years—the first pizzeria was established in New York in 1895—what had been a slice of nostalgia in the diet of an immigrant minority has become one of the most popular dishes in American cuisine. And, unlike what has happened in other countries, pizza is not only cooked and served in thousands of pizzerias, but it has also become part of American home cooking. In *The Fannie Farmer Cookbook,* for example, there are no fewer than five extremely detailed recipes for pizza. And it is a pleasure to note that, aside from a few variations based on distinctive American customs and the availability of ingredients, these are recipes that fully respect the Italian notions of the pizza. I must note, though, that for a long while the recipes rarely included garlic. But they do now, since the use of garlic in American cooking has skyrocketed in recent years. Thank goodness. 99

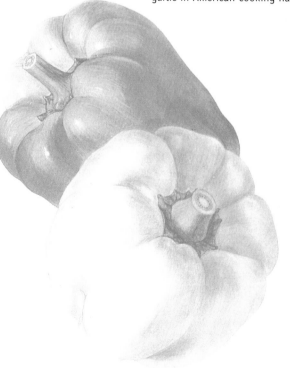

PIZZA AL GORGONZOLA E ANANAS—PIZZA WITH GORGONZOLA CHEESE AND PINEAPPLE

As odd as the flavor combination may seem, this pizza actually derives directly from the traditional combination of tart and sweet that in the past dominated many of the cuisines of the Western world. Even so, many pizza chefs in Italy call this the "Pizza Esotica." The counterpoint between the rotund yet slightly harsh flavor of the gorgonzola cheese and the sweet yet bracing taste of the pineapple creates a roller-coaster of inviting tastes and sensations, underscored by the soft and tasty flavor of the crust. Ooh la la! A pizza that needs to be tasted to be believed.

The Pizza al Gorgonzola e Ananas calls for a slightly sweet white wine with a marked and persistent aroma—wines such as the Orvieto Classico or the Recioto di Gambellara. The ideal accompaniment, however, is the Moscato Spumante.

RECIPE

1 pettola (see page 58)
¼ cup/50 mL gorgonzola, (not spicy)
½ cup/125 mL pineapple chunks, fresh or canned

Distribute the gorgonzola over the crust, cut the pineapple into small pieces, and arrange it over the pizza. Put it in the oven and bake for approximately 15 minutes at 450°F (230°C).

In the fall of 1975 I had just returned to Milan after living abroad for fifteen years. I came back to a homeland where I felt completely out of place. Everything had changed, and not just politically and culturally. The food had changed too, and not always for the better. I realized this when old friends I had not seen for years would invite me to dine with them in restaurants that served improbable and pretentious dishes.

In my efforts to discover any interesting new developments, I tried to alternate my samplings between the traditional cooking of times gone and (often disconcerting) the new cuisine that was emerging. So I was pleased when a friend invited me to have dinner with him at a pizzeria near the Stazione Centrale, the main rail station of Milan. The pizzeria featured a repertoire of both traditional and newer pizzas. The owner was a cultured gentleman, who was happy to talk about the state of Italian cuisine. He suggested I try the Pizza al Gorgonzola e Ananas, pizza with gorgonzola cheese and pineapple, accompanied by a bottle of Orvieto Classico. "If you don't like it," he reassured me, "we will bring you any other pizza you care to order in its place." Though I had my doubts, I must honestly confess that after the first few bites I recognized what a great pizza it truly was.

At the end of the meal, the owner came by my table and told me that back home—he was from Broni, in the Oltrepò Pavese—it was traditional to eat gorgonzola cheese with the sweet and super-bubbly Moscato that their vintners produced. In light of that fact, the contrast between the sharp flavor of the cheese and the sweet taste of the pineapple no longer seemed so odd, and indeed it would have been perfect if combined with a good glass of Moscato. I later decided to test that hypothesis, and I can confirm that the vintners of the Oltrepò Pavese know their business.

AN OVEN MADE OF CLAY

Among the many factors that contribute to the status of the pizza as a little masterpiece of the culinary art is the oven in which it is baked. With all due respect for technological progress, there is nothing that cooks a pizza better than a wood-burning oven. And it is not just a question of temperature: the slight traces of ash that cling to the base of the pizza, the almost imperceptible nuances of flavor and aroma created by the smoke, and the vapors that are released from the burning wood all add a little intangible something that gives a special quality to the taste and smell of true pizza.

The wood-burning oven described here is a replica of those which our distant ancestors used to bake what I described as "proto-pizzas" in Chapter 1. The oven is still quite common along the Ionian coast of Greece, where it is used for cooking roasts, pies, cakes, and focaccia.

As you can see from the instructions that follow, such an oven is not at all complicated to build. If you have enough outdoor space, why not build a wood-burning oven in which you can cook the splendid pizzas of tradition, along with tasty meats and fish?

First of all, you should choose an appropriate location.

You will need a flat, level area, roughly 80 x 80 inches (2 x 2 m) that is at least a foot or two from any adjacent buildings. You should choose an area clear of bushes, shrubbery, or trees, which might be damaged by the heat of the oven, the smoke, or the occasional spray of sparks.

Carefully level a surface of 60 x 60 inches (1.5 x 1.5 m), within the larger area you have marked out. If the soil is crumbly or rocky, it is best to prepare a solid and safe foundation that can easily support the weight of the finished oven. For that purpose, dig a recessed area, 63 x 63 inches (1.6 x 1.6 m) in area, some 4 inches (10 cm) deep, which you then fill with concrete. Once the base is ready, you should proceed to build two low parallel walls, using perforated bricks, laid flat. (Make sure you use heat-resistant bricks.) Each low wall should be about 40 inches long and 36 inches high (100 cm long and 90 cm high); the distance between the two walls, measured from the exterior (including the thickness of the bricks), should be 40 inches (100 cm).

The next step is to connect the two low walls with a flat load-bearing platform; this will support the oven. For this purpose, you need to spread fresh mortar on the tops of the two low walls and, starting at a distance of 2 inches (5 cm) from the far ends, at intervals of 6 inches (15 cm), lay 7 round steel bars, with diameters ranging from $3/16$ to $5/16$ of an inch (5 to 8 mm), 40 inches (100 cm) in length, connecting the two low walls.

The load-bearing platform is made of refractories—or firebricks—laid flat and cemented with heat-resistant mortar. Once you have laid all the bricks, cover the platform with a thin layer of mortar, and then cover the whole surface with another layer of clay roughly $3/8$ of an inch (1 cm) deep; level and smooth this layer. The clay used for this layer is the same clay used in the construction of the oven— it should be thinned with 10 percent of very fine sand, and thoroughly washed, since the exact quantity of sand depends on the quality of the clay. Make sure you consult with your supplier. Once you have readied the load-bearing platform, you can proceed to the construction of the oven itself, which is built with the technique known in Italian as "a colombina." This is a very ancient technique, involving the preparation of long rolled lengths of wet clay, slightly thicker than the final desired thickness that—in this case—is about 1 inch (2.5 cm). The lengths of clay are then arranged in a three-dimensional spiral, rising row over row, not unlike a beehive; you press each length of clay atop the one beneath it, and then pound on the joints between them with a broad, not too heavy hammer while supporting the structure from within with the palm of the free hand. Since it is not physically possible to do the whole

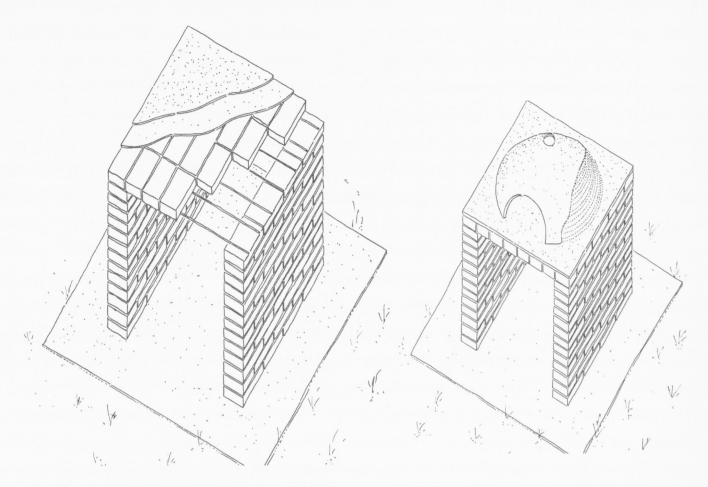

job with a single length of rolled clay, you join the various lengths of clay to each other by moistening the ends and then pressing them together. To ensure the coiled lengths adhere one layer to the next, moisten the surface with a little water when laying each length atop the one beneath it. The oven itself consists of a hollow hemisphere of clay, built as described, with an internal diameter of about 32 inches (80 cm) and a wall about ¾ inch (2 cm) thick. To obtain a symmetrical configuration, you can use two templates: one for the base, consisting of a circle made of any material, with an inner diameter—corresponding to the external diameter of the oven—of about 33 inches (82 cm).

To check the uniformity of the oven's external wall, use a template comprising a quarter circumference, with an inner diameter equal to that of the circular template. While you are building the oven, make sure that there are no bubbles of air trapped between the coils of clay or at the joints linking together the lengths of rolled clay. Any such air bubbles will expand during the successive "seasonings" of the oven and cause cracking and shattering. The way to eliminate the bubbles is with the hammering procedure described above. Do this task very thoroughly: the best results are obtained when the partially dried clay takes on the rough consistency of leather. To prevent the clay from drying unevenly, cover the structure with wet rags whenever you have to stop work. When you have worked your way up to the top of the oven structure, leave a circular opening at the very top, some 4 inches (about 10 cm) in diameter;

this serves as a chimney. Once the structure is complete, you can cut the mouth of the oven out with a thin steel wire, stretched tight, as if you were cutting cheese or polenta. Use a sharp knife to gently cut an opening for your hand roughly in the middle of where the door is to go. Then take an end of the wire in each hand and lightly "saw" back and forth with wire to cut out the door to the desired size and shape. The mouth of the oven should be about 16 inches (40 cm) wide and some 8 inches (20 cm) tall.

Once completed, let the oven dry for at least a week, during which time you can fill in any cracks or fissures that may develop with a semi-liquid mixture of clay and water called "barbottina" in Italian. Once the structure is completely dry, you can begin to "cook" or "season" the oven by lighting a

small, weak fire inside it. After it has cooled completely make another, slightly larger, fire. Gradually make the fires higher and hotter (with complete coolings between each) until the entire external surface has taken on a more-or-less intense reddish-yellow color, a color that will vary depending on the degree of seasoning but also on the quality of the clay. You can repair any fissures or cracks that develop during the seasoning, with more "barbottina." However, you can only add the "barbottina" when the oven has cooled completely. If the draw in the oven is too strong or too weak, you can reduce (by adding clay) or enlarge (by sanding) the mouth or the chimney of the oven.

If properly stoked, the oven can easily be maintained at 650°F (350°C)—the ideal temperature for baking good pizzas.

NUNC EST

BIBENDUM

OR, IF YOU PREFER, RAISE YOUR GLASS

3

" True pizza

deserves to be eaten

with beverages

that enhance the diner's

pleasure and underscore

the flavors and aromas

of these marvels

of Italian folk cuisine . . .

UNC EST BIBENDUM

OR, IF YOU PREFER, RAISE YOUR GLASS

A few general guidelines

True pizzas deserve to be eaten with beverages that enhance the diner's pleasure and underscore the flavors and aromas of these marvels of Italian folk cuisine. But it should really come as no surprise that a beverage tradition didn't develop along with the pizzas themselves. We should not forget that the growth in popularity of the pizza as we now know it began (as we saw in the first chapter) at the end of the eighteenth century. And despite the fact that at least two of the crowned heads of Europe made no secret of their fondness for a good pizza, for a long time the main consumers of this savory dish were the poorer elements of society—people who could certainly appreciate a good glass of wine, but who probably couldn't afford it very often.

Be that as it may, we are left with the fact that while pizza is now one of the most popular dishes on earth, no connoisseur has yet addressed the issue of what wines to drink with which pizzas. Wine writers, vintners, and even chefs have been remiss in not addressing this rather obvious subject. Certainly some pizzerias offer a limited wine list, but the choices available usually have little to do with pizza. I've met very few waiters who felt it worthwhile to suggest what to drink with a particular pizza. This is a real pity because while pizzas often manage to withstand the wrong beverage, a well-chosen accompaniment can truly enhance the pizza's gratification of the palate.

Happily, this situation can be resolved by applying a few rules of thumb and by following some simple suggestions, which I offer below.

First, I have to say that the best accompaniment for a pizza is wine—a good, properly selected wine. And for several reasons. To start, no other beverage can match the flavors and perfumes that pizzas offer. Second, consider the bold flavors and lingering aftertastes from some typical pizza ingredients, for example, the anchovies in the Pizza Napoletana and the onions in a Pizza Pugliese. When you remember that the taking of wine between mouthfuls of food eliminates or reduces lingering tastes and aftertastes, you understand why wine is so ideal an accompaniment. No monotony on the palate, and you can experience each new mouthful of pizza as if for the first time.

Now we must ask the obvious question: which wine with which pizza? Let me establish

a few basic points of reference. Keep clearly in mind that the flavors and aromas of pizza are always lively and direct, and that it is always possible—and always best—to select wines with an equally lively flavor. Young wines are often the most suitable. They are capable of expressing immediately—at the first sip—all of the warmth of a sunny vineyard. Despite popular wisdom, I believe the wines should never be too dry or tannic (except in exceptional circumstances). Otherwise, you lose a lot of the wonderfully contrasting effects of a good pizza. So it's really necessary to write off—however reluctantly—many great full-bodied Italian wines.

Next, the "style" of the wine, as much as the taste, serves to underscore the overall flavors of the various ingredients of the pizza as well as to free the palate of lingering aftertastes. Either a "still" wine (clear and tranquil, free of carbon dioxide bubbles) or a "lively" wine (semi-sparkling to fully sparkling) can be well matched with a pizza. Those who prefer "lively" wines will find sparkling wines that can splendidly accompany a great variety of pizzas, both among the wines that are "lively" by tradition (such as Lambrusco, Freisa, Buttafuoco, and the

Malvasia Secca dei Colli di Parma) and among those that have become "lively" through new techniques developed by modern enologists (young Barberas, certain Pinots, or some of the Chardonnays).

Spumante proper deserves a special discussion. The idea of serving a folk dish like pizza with a "vino nobile" like Spumante is unquestionably tempting. All the same, we must simply resign ourselves to the fact that the Spumantes obtained through a second fermentation in the bottle—the Brut—are too dry and too delicately aromatic to be freely set beside just any pizza. (But there are some interesting exceptions, as we shall see.) On the other hand, the Spumantes made with a second fermentation in an autoclave are characterized by a less dry flavor and a more marked aroma. Given their specific characteristics, these Spumantes (such as Prosecco or Cartizze) offer some very interesting combinations with pizzas.

And, last, a crucial question—red wine or white wine?

Even though white wines generally feature tastes and bouquets that make them ideal accompaniments for many types of pizza, there is no lack of red wines that are just as well suited to certain kinds of pizza. A few examples in the following list of suggestions will illustrate this point. But keep in mind that my suggestions are meant to serve primarily as examples to help you identify wines that are best suited for particular pizzas. I should also tell you that these examples are limited—for perhaps obvious considerations of national pride—to just a few of the many splendid Italian wines that can make it even more enjoyable to eat a well-made pizza.

What to drink with seafood pizzas: . . . Pizza Napoletana, or Neapolitan-Style Pizza . . .

Let us begin with the best-known pizza, the classic Pizza Napoletana and its close relatives, the Pizza alla Siciliana, and the Piscialandrea and the Sardenaira of western Liguria. In all four cases, the dominant component of the flavor is the intense taste of the anchovies or the sardines, a flavor of fish (further sharpened in the Pizza alla Siciliana by the salty capers) that immediately suggests combining it with a fine white wine. Be careful, however. These flavors are so powerful that many of the excellent white wines that one would normally serve with fish and shellfish could take on an unpleasant metallic aftertaste that may spoil the dining experience. Therefore, it is best to select a white wine that is dry to moderately sweet, delicately fruity, and pleasantly perfumed. Try, for example the Castelli Romani or the Malvasia Secca dei Colli di Parma, or perhaps a Chardonnay, with an improbable scent of bananas. These suggestions might seem to rule red wines out entirely; and yet, because of a piece of alchemistic legerdemain that is difficult, if not impossible, to explain, the Rossese di Dolceacqua and the Cerasuolo di Vittoria—two wines with radically different features—manage to work perfectly with the pungent flavor of anchovies and sardines, at first rounding off and softening that taste, and then finally eliminating it at a pleasantly gradual pace.

... Pizza alla Pescatora, or Fisherman-Style Pizza ...

Most of the variations on the Pizza alla Pescatora—the pizza with "frutti di mare"—permit moderately dry white wines, savory and bone dry, pleasantly perfumed. Wines such as Vermentino della Gallura—or better yet its compatriot S'eleme—or else Cinque Terre, Greco di Tufo, or Martina Franca all fit the bill. For a special occasion, consider a Prosecco or a Cartizze, certainly more imposing but, precisely because of the bubbliness, capable of eliminating any persistent aftertaste.

... Pizza all'Anguilla, or Pizza with Smoked Eel ...

The Pizza all'Anguilla, both because it contains smoked eel and because it uses tomato, goes well with white wine. It would be wise to select a very dry wine with a fairly marked perfume. Wines like Trebbiano di Romagna or Verdicchio Classico dei Castelli di Jesi, with a pleasingly bitterish aftertaste, nicely counterpoint the sweeter taste of the eel. Or try a Bianco d'Alcamo with its neutral bouquet but a fresh and fruity taste, or a fresh and bone-dry Bianco di Breganze. The Pizza all'Anguilla, with its interesting flavor and appearance, also goes extremely well with certain special reds, such as Lambrusco, especially the bone-dry variety. The San Colombano, with its almondy aftertaste, pleasingly overlays the combined flavors of eel and tomato. Or try the Buttafuoco dell'Oltrepò Pavese, for its delicate perfume.

What to drink with other pizzas ...

Of course, when the flavor and aroma of the pizza smack of dry land, the wine accompaniment becomes a relatively straightforward matter. The absence of dominant salty or fishy tastes and aromas considerably broadens the range of appropriate selections from both reds and whites. Wine selections based on the particular flavors and aromas of the various types of pizza will make for some noteworthy alliances at your table.

... the Margherita Pizza ...

Take the Pizza Margherita, which offers the palate a harmonious blend of flavors and scents without a single dominant or discordant note. This quality can be highlighted by a white wine with a bone-dry taste or even, perhaps, a semi-sparkling wine such as the Blanc de Morgex et de la Salle—a great wine from Valle d'Aosta, which with its slightly tart flavor contrasts nicely with the sweeter tastes of the mozzarella and the tomato. Or try a Bianco di Pitigliano, with its bitterish aftertaste, or, for those who eschew anything too complex, a Bianchello del Metauro.

Among the reds you would do well to choose a Taurasi—not too old, however, lest the full and bone-dry flavor becomes austere—or a Cirò. If you prefer livelier flavors, try a young Barbera, perhaps sparkling, or even a Freisa (dry or sweetish)—one of the favorite wines of the Queen after whom this pizza was named. With the Pizza Margherita you may also drink a Spumante Brut, not out of adulation for the pizza's royal pedigree but because, in this case, the delicate bouquet of the wine will underscore the sophisticated tones of the ingredients, while the dry taste and the titillation of the bubbles will mitigate almost entirely the inevitable aftertaste, which might otherwise become tiresome.

. . . Pizza alla Pugliese, or Apulian-Style Pizza . . .

A Spumante Brut, strange to say, makes excellent company for a Pizza alla Pugliese, especially if the pizza is made in the oldest version, without potatoes, but with a generous dusting of black pepper. Even if flavored with "caciocavallo" or pecorino cheese, the dominant taste and scent are those of the onions—sweet and soft—and these are properly enhanced by the dryness of the wine. If you don't choose a Spumante, there's no lack of alternatives. As far as whites are concerned, you may find perfect accompaniments with wines that have a fresh and fruity flavor, such as a Müller Thurgau, or a slightly bitter flavor, such as the Riesling Trentino, which would nicely counterpoint the flavors of the onion and the cheese.

Among the red wines, tradition demands the Primitivo di Manduria, soft and powerful, but you can also rely on less imposing but equally vigorous wines, such as a Sardinian Cannonau, a Cacce e Mitte di Lucera, or even a Nobile di Montepulciano, similar to a Chianti, but less tannic.

Certain traits call for certain measures . . .

You will want a red wine for any of those pizzas in which red chili pepper makes its biting presence known, or for a Pizza ai Quattro Formaggi (four-cheese pizza). In these cases, the palate must cope with pleasant, savory tastes, but tastes that nonetheless make every effort to rule the roost. You will want a wine with a certain body, with a mellow flavor; and since these are pizzas that encourage one to drink, you should not choose particularly strong wines. Some suitable varieties include a Lago di Caldaro (or, if you prefer, a Kalterersee), a Refosco, a Valpolicella, or a Dolcetto or, even, a Grignolino, with a slightly bitter but pleasing aftertaste. But there is a broad array of possibilities among the white wines as well. These rather unusual pizzas, in fact, go perfectly with wines such as a Bianco di Custoza, Pinot Grigio, Tocai—from Friuli or Lombardy—or a Bianco della Valdinievole; these last three are often perfect in the lovely semi-sparkling versions.

And then there are the many pizzas that feature vegetables, almost always accompanied by mozzarella and, in some cases, by ham or prosciutto. White or red wines with the general characteristics mentioned above (medium body, soft, balanced flavor) will provide an excellent accompaniment; but if you wish, you can also find some extraordinary combinations by playing on the features of the vegetables used.

For pizzas ennobled with mushrooms—and especially porcini mushrooms—you may once again rely on the Spumante Brut. The prevalent taste is that of the mushrooms, slightly sweet and earthy, accompanied by a distinctive aroma that intensifies with every bite. Rather than trying to overpower the mushrooms, it is best to enhance them with a delicate, yet persistent, aroma. The dryness together with the bubbles should offset any excessive aftertastes. You can obtain the same effect from any fine white wine having a velvety flavor and an understated bouquet; wines such as the Cortese—excellent Cortese del Monferrato with its slightly bitter undertone—the Pinot, the Sauvignon, the Locorotondo, or the Greco. And, since mushrooms go well with a full-bodied wine, we should not overlook those red wines that can turn the meal into a truly memorable event. For this purpose, I strongly recommend two wines that deserve to be more popular: the Faro, made in the area

around Messina, and the Donnici, originally from the Cosenza area. Or try the Cesanese, which boasts an extremely fine, slightly bitter undertaste—not unlike a young Cabernet, with its fantastic grassy bouquet.

If it's a pizza with artichokes that you're enjoying, such as the Pizza Quattro Stagioni or Pizza Capricciosa, then keep in mind the refined and sweet aftertaste that is so typical of the vegetable. If the predominant flavor is that of artichoke, you would not want a wine that clashes with it of course. The best idea, then, is to ignore the reds entirely and choose a white wine. Look for features that underscore both the taste and the aftertaste of the pizza. Try whites such as a Tocai Italico, or a Montefiascone, an Orvieto, a Malvasia Secca dei Colli di Parma, or even a neighboring Val Nure dei Colli Piacentini; this last wine, if semi-sparkling, is a particularly interesting accompaniment. Allow me to say just a few more words about the ideal accompaniment for a pizza with artichokes. There are purists who might argue that the ideal beverage for artichokes that have not been fried (as is usually the case with pizza)

is water, which enhances and preserves the delightful sweet aftertaste of this splendid vegetable. Those purists certainly have a point. However, with pizza, one needs to consider the presence of the mozzarella, which when cooked demands a drink that can bring out its finest qualities.

Though I don't offer a recipe for it, the Pizza agli Asparagi, or pizza with asparagus, suggests two good accompaniments. The pizza's dominant flavor—a product of the combined flavors of eggs, asparagus, and Parmesan cheese—is soft, rotund, slightly sweet, and even touched with the faintest hint of a scent of grass. One might therefore select a white wine with a velvety flavor and slight bouquet, such as a Pinot Bianco, a Verduzzo, a Marino—dry or sweetish, according to preference—or a Bianco di Ischia. The other possibility is to accompany this refined pizza with an equally noble wine: a Spumante Brut, which will help to eliminate any aftertastes, precisely because of its elegant bubbliness. For pizzas with fresh vegetables one should select a red wine with a savory flavor. There are many potential candidates, ranging from Barbera—either a classic Barbera, or a

young and semi-sparkling one—to Lambrusco, Bonarda, Rosso Conero, Sangiovese, and Merlot.

A surprising combination . . .

Another suggestion that may at first seem odd, but which is based on culinary and enological traditions, is for the proper wine to accompany the unique Pizza al Gorgonzola e Ananas (pizza with gorgonzola cheese and pineapple). For me, the most successful accompaniment is none other than a Moscato Spumante Naturale—a wine that of course would also work well with the Pizza ai Quattro Formaggi (pizza with four cheeses) whenever the dominant flavor is that of the gorgonzola. At first blush, this accompaniment may seem to challenge conventions, but in fact it is heir to an old tradition once common throughout the area known as the Oltrepò Pavese, which calls for gorgonzola to be matched with Moscato Dolce, an aromatic and joyously sparkling local wine. The delicately sweet flavor of the Moscato serves as an unaffected counterpoint to the pungency of the gorgonzola and the decidedly sharp taste of the pineapple, while its softly aromatic bouquet will eliminate all the aftertastes so typical of the two ingredients. On the same basis, you can make

other selections to accompany this pizza (or other pizzas like it) with wines such as a Recioto di Gambellara or a sweetish Malvasia dei Colli di Parma ("amabile," as the Italian would have it)—to name just two great white wines. Among the reds, try a good Lambrusco or a sweetish Freisa, or else, staying in the Oltrepò Pavese region, a Sangue di Giuda. Another worthy accompaniment is the Vernaccia di Oristano, drier than any of the other suggested wines, but pleasant and with an underlying taste that is just slightly bitter, which contrasts elegantly with the flavors in the crust and the other ingredients. The remarkable bouquet of this superb wine will eliminate any excessively persistent aftertaste.

A few final suggestions about wine . . .

Allow me now to offer a few final considerations. First, let me say once again that the various wines listed should be considered as examples, and not directives. Different factors—notably, geography—may make it difficult to find specific selections on the wine lists of many pizzerias and restaurants. But there is nothing wrong in choosing a wine with similar characteristics to the wines suggested here; and that is

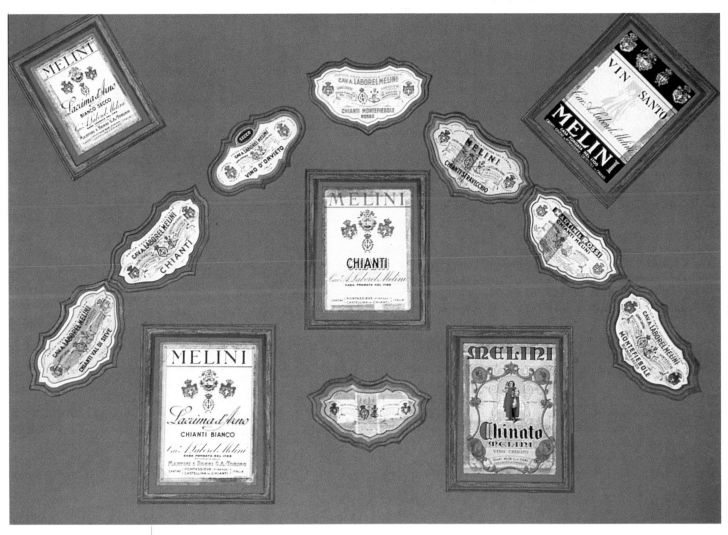

Collection of antique wine
labels

always possible, given the variety of Italian wines. Don't think, either, that you must choose only a pedigreed wine. Before you turn down a carafe of "house wine" or "vino della casa," it would be best to taste that wine with care: you might be in for a very pleasant surprise. Last of all, remember that these suggestions for the best combinations of pizza and wine provide a guide at best. The final choice should be based on your own preferences. In other words, it is better to drink a wine that you like, even if it is not perfectly "suited" to the pizza that you are tasting, than to force down a wine that you are not particularly fond of simply to follow blindly the dictates of an overweening gourmand such as myself. One more general piece of advice, this one concerning the temperature of the wine that you serve with pizza. If it is a white wine, it should be cool or slightly chilled, but never cold, lest you numb your palate and limit its ability to enjoy both flavor and aroma. A red wine, especially a young and lively red, should be cellar cool, or at the very lowest, a few degrees below room temperature. Only the great red wines should be served at temperatures of around 65 to 68 degrees Fahrenheit. A semi-sparkling is most enjoyable when slightly chilled.

Pizza with beer

An alternative to wine is beer, which is not at all a poor cousin or second choice. Indeed, a carefully selected beer can make an ideal accompaniment to most of the pizzas I know. I trust that this statement will not offend purists who insist that pizzas be served with wine and with wine alone. We should not forget that beer originated and became popular—probably even earlier than wine —in the southwestern area of the Mediterranean basin, and that it was not until much later that beer became common in northern Europe, where climate has prevented the cultivation of grapevines. I should also point out that the basic, pleasantly bitter and relatively persistent taste of a good beer, along with the soft aroma of malt from the foam, serves as a marvelous counterpoint to most of the flavors and scents that make a pizza so appetizing. The beer can also eliminate certain powerful aftertastes. Another point in beer's favor is that for some years now very good non-alcoholic varieties have been on the market. This is a significant development because those who do not drink alcohol can enjoy a fine pizza without having to settle for just water.

I believe, however, that the dark or heavily malted beers, as well as the stouts, should be ruled out. Too strong an aroma of malt, in fact, would overwhelm the similar—but far more delicate—aroma of the crust, and would clash with the ingredients. The elevated malt content gives these heavier beers a taste that tends toward bittersweet; it's stupendous when you are just hanging out with friends, but it's poorly suited to the rough and slightly aggressive flavors of most pizzas.

What beer should you choose?

Choose beers that are pleasantly bitter from the hops, fragrant with malt, and crowned by a white head. But once again, the big question: which beers with which pizzas?

The concepts that should guide us in our selection are the same as with wine, even though they are applied to different properties.

Pizzas that feature the sharp and pungent flavors of anchovies or sardines should be accompanied by beers with low malt content and a none-too-bitter taste—as is the case with many Scandinavian beers—in order to avoid excessively sharp contrasts. With the Pizza alla Pescatora (fisherman-style pizza), or the Pizza all'Anguilla (pizza with smoked eel), you should choose fuller-bodied beers, such as German or Dutch beers, or those made in Belgium or northern France. Despite their high malt content, these beers have a persistent bitter taste that, with the abundant foam, merges perfectly with the shifting tastes and surprising aromas of these remarkable pizzas.

Beer is at its best with a pizza that features salami among its ingredients, though we should distinguish among the types of salami. For example, to enjoy a nice piece of Pizza Bianca properly stuffed with mortadella or prosciutto, you should choose a bitterish beer with a fine

head, but as little malt as possible. On the other hand, for pizzas that have the traditional baked salami—such as the Pizza Capricciosa or the Pizza al Prosciutto e ai Funghi—you should choose a more full-bodied beer, less bitter and more aromatic. This choice will nicely emphasize the particular flavor that salami acquires after baking, while helping to eliminate a distinctive aftertaste that can, after a while, turn unpleasant.

Considerably more complex is the question of finding the right beer for a pizza with vegetables among its main ingredients. In the case of fresh vegetables, the balancing effect of the mozzarella favors beers that are not too bitter or aromatic: lighter beers, usually quite blond in color. A Pizza agli Asparagi (pizza with asparagus) goes well—because of the eggs—with a sharply malted beer that isn't too bitter. This enhances the gentle taste and delicate aroma of the asparagus. Again, if you find yourself facing a pizza with artichokes, apply the same guidelines as for the Pizza agli Asparagi. In the Pizza ai Carciofi e ai Funghi—or pizza with artichokes and mushrooms—the tomato plays an important role, so you will want a slightly bitter beer with a pronounced aroma. This will result in a combination

that you will long remember with pleasure.

You may at some point find yourself sure of the beer you want and then wonder which "style" is best: draft, bottled, or canned beer. Aside from the question of availability, this is primarily a matter of whether you prefer a more or a less foamy beer. Draft beer tends to preserve its "head"—the thick layer of bright white foam that so embellishes a glass or a mug—for a longer time; bottled beers lose their head more quickly; and canned beer is the first to lose the head. So although the same brand of beer may be of the same quality, different containers produce different levels of pressure (highest in the barrel, lowest in the can), which, by the laws of physics, create different levels of soluble carbon dioxide in the liquid. The taste and the aroma, of course, remain essentially the same, and there is still the titillating release of tiny bubbles with every sip.

Another matter of preference is temperature. Let me offer only one piece of advice: good beers shouldn't be served too cold and never icy.

In Great Britain and Ireland, where beer is the national drink, it is served at room temperature. This may seem odd, but the same rule applied to wine also applies to beer. Excessively low temperatures will not allow the palate to appreciate the nuances in taste and aroma.

Some beverages to avoid . . .

This chapter would not be complete without some mention of the beverages that you should not drink with a fine pizza. All pizzas share certain natural flavors and aromas, direct and intense, which ill withstand the accompaniment of drinks with artificial and overpowering tastes and smells. Such beverages, especially if they are heavily carbonated, overwhelm the palate and cancel out all other sensations. Here, too, the golden rule on individual preferences applies, but—when it comes to certain choices—we must only smile politely when colas and such other concoctions of bubbly water and sugar are allowed to depreciate the value of otherwise exquisite pizzas.

BEYOND THE

YEAR 2000

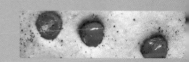

66 **The time has come, then,**

to offer some predictions

concerning the future

of pizza . . .

BEYOND THE YEAR 2000

Pizzerias in New York, Moscow, and Beijing

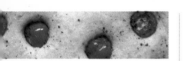

The current situation

In the previous chapters, I covered briefly the fascinating story of the evolutionary process that transformed the archaic votive barley cake—a rude dough, unleavened, smeared with fat or oil—into the pizzas we now know and love. The history of pizza wends its way from the Neolithic period on, and it parallels the larger story of the evolution of the human race, nebulous at first, fragmentary and slow, and then in time becoming increasingly precise and rapid as we approach the present, and finally—over the past hundred years—moving at dizzying speed.

The time has come, then, to offer some predictions on the future of pizza; in my estimation we shall see some interesting developments. Making predictions is a risky venture, so let me first elaborate on the present state of affairs.

In its present form, pizza dates back nearly two hundred years, the product of a long culinary evolution. It came about as a solution to the problem of how to provide nourishing but cheap food for the poor and the very poor who lived in the streets and alleys of Naples. It was an invention that took its inspiration from the great tradition of focaccia and earlier proto-pizzas. It achieved its full flowering only when the tomato became part of Italian cuisine some 200 years ago. This invention was so successful that the pizza won a following beyond the narrow confines in which it developed, and eventually spread throughout Italy and, in time, the world. This astonishing success is remarkable in two ways.

First, the basic concept of pizza has been accepted everywhere, almost without variation. This is especially true of the pizzerias and among the major food manufacturers. There are, and there always will be, variations in the ingredients, but these are generally modifications prompted by availability problems or else by special tastes and dietary customs in a certain region. In other words, in Nairobi just as in Oslo, in Capetown just as in Glasgow, in Lansing just as in Moscow, in Freemantle (Australia) just as in Buenos Aires—to mention just a few of my own personal experiences—the mechanics of preparing the "pettola," the rapid scattering of

ingredients over its surface, the baking process, and even the equipment used by the pizza chef are all nearly exactly the same as what the pizzerias of Naples have used for the past two centuries.

The loss of national identity

Second, "pizza" has directly entered into virtually every language on earth, but even the Italian colloquial expression—"andiamo a farci una pizza," or "let's go get ourselves a pizza" (the literal translation)—has become part of spoken language everywhere, with the same meaning: let's go have an informal, friendly meal. Pizza is now part of the culinary and social cultures of numerous countries. In the English-speaking world, and especially in the United States, there is now the phenomenon of the "pizza party," a somewhat rowdy affair centered around what else. Pizza's adaptability to different countries and cultures is certainly an interesting and multifaceted phenomenon, though it is not entirely positive. There is a risk that in certain places pizza eventually will lose its proper national identity. Because of its widespread appeal in North America, it is in danger of losing its association with Italian folk cuisine. In America, the massive presence of pizzerias has stripped the pizza of folk connotations that once hinted of something approaching exoticism—that once made the pizza something new, something original. In other

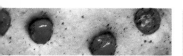

words, pizza, even though its culinary structure has remained substantially unvaried, is now considered a distinctly American food. The newer generations are forgetting its origins. (Among the newer generations I also include the descendants of those Italians who immigrated to America between the end of the nineteenth century and the first few decades of the twentieth century.) So many people of Italian heritage are now fourth- or fifth-generation Americans, completely integrated into U.S. society. Slowly their ties to their ancient homeland are weakening and breaking.

Pre-packaged pizzas-in-a-box, with pre-measured ingredients

The phenomenon of the denationalization of pizza in North America and elsewhere has been underway for a number of decades and is probably irreversible. In this connection I remember a strange encounter I had about twenty years ago. I spent at least half an hour unsuccessfully trying to persuade a young Canadian girl, a friend of my daughter's, that pizza was not American. In other countries that have been invaded by pizza the process of assimilation has certainly been less complete, but if the current universal popularity of pizza is any indication, we cannot rule out the possibility that this inexpensive food, invented to feed the "lazzaroni" (the poverty-stricken and hungry of Naples, so-called after the freshly risen, but horribly ragged, Lazarus), should one day become the world food par excellence.

The advent of the packaged pizza

Another factor that affects the present state of affairs of the pizza is the penetration of major food manufacturers into a field that was once dominated by individual artisans. The inter-

Ready-to-bake pizza

est of major food producers is easily explained by the skyrocketing growth in pizza consumption and by the need for new products, given the saturation of the market by other types of pre-packaged foods.

In Italy, the earliest attempts at marketing packaged pizzas date back at least thirty years. The packages contained all, or nearly all, of the pre-measured ingredients needed for making one or two pizzas of the classic varieties. The formula was simple: each box contained flour and yeast, as well as a little measuring cup for the water and the oil used in making the dough; one then simply followed the detailed instructions on how to make the dough and then bake the pie.

These packages had the great advantage of leaving ample freedom to personalize the pizzas, but they necessarily relied on not-always adequate skills for

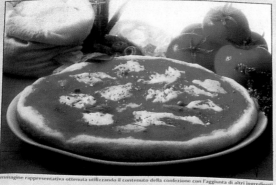

BasiPizza
Pronto forno

La confezione contiene 2 basi di pasta per pizza

Basi Pizza
Per alimenti
480 g ℮

SERVIZIO CORTESIA

167-848020

Immagine rappresentativa ottenuta utilizzando il contenuto della confezione con l'aggiunta di altri ingredienti

Preparato per pizza a lievitazione naturale.

Preparazione: Accendete il forno e portatelo a 230° C. Non utilizzare il forno a microonde. Mettete le basi in teglie unte in precedenza o su fogli di carta da forno. Mettete in una scodella della polpa di pomodoro (circa 200 g per 2 basi), insaporite con olio e sale e distribuitela sulle basi. Guarnite a piacere con mozzarella, prosciutto, funghetti, olive... e tutti gli ingredienti che stuzzicano la vostra fantasia. Infornate a metà altezza, lasciate cuocere per circa 10 minuti, quindi insaporite con un pizzico di origano e servite subito a tavola.
Da consumarsi preferibilmente

An electric pizza oven

making the "pettola," or crust. The results, partly because of the inadequate home ovens of the period, were often disappointing. I still sadly remember certain "homemade" pizzas that were virtually inedible—there were a few rather dreary toppings on a crust that had been reduced to a sort of hard biscuit. This type of product did not enjoy much success because of the unpredictability of the results and the amount of time required for preparation. The food industry has since developed a new generation of products that rely on the improved techniques of preservation, transportation, and distribution. These pre-cooked products are pizzas that are complete in nearly every way. They are either vacuum packed and sold "fresh," and thus can be stored only for short periods; or they are partially pre-cooked and frozen for long-term conservation. These pizzas can be reheated in a normal home oven or in a microwave oven.

While the timing and the temperatures for the final heating are clearly marked on the package, there is often no hint that it would be a good idea to sprinkle the surface of the pizza with a little olive oil before placing it in the oven. This procedure, as pizza chefs know full well, allows for a better distribution of flavors, and, above all, keeps the pizza pleasantly soft, even when it has not been baked perfectly.

Some food manufacturers also supply pre-cooked pizzas to many takeout outlets that do not have the equipment to prepare pizzas from scratch on site. Alongside these mass-produced pizzas are those prepared directly by supermarkets, making use of partially pre-cooked crusts—likewise mass produced—upon which the various ingredients are then laid out. These products are wrapped in a plastic film once they are ready and then kept cool for relatively short periods; they are not, however, frozen. To eat one all you have to do is unwrap it and heat it in the oven—a matter of minutes.

While subject to improvement, these mass-produced pizzas allow people to enjoy

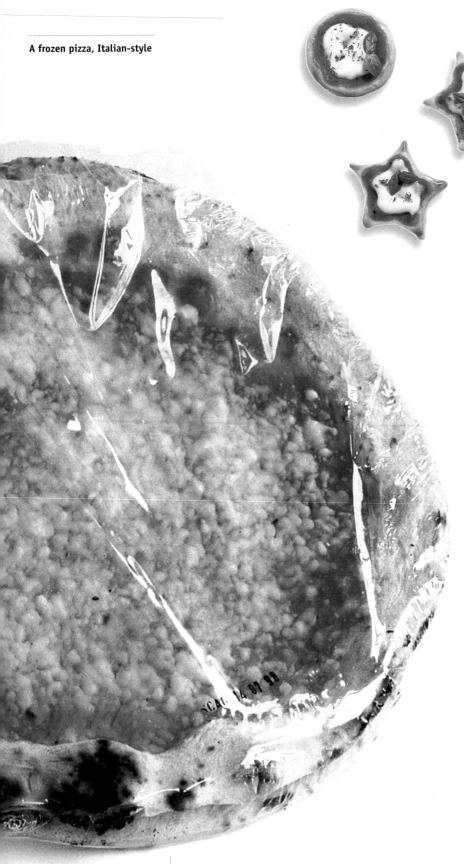

A frozen pizza, Italian-style

pizzas that, by and large, are of satisfactory quality. Because of the ease and speed with which they can be prepared, these products have gained enormous popularity. All the same, it is the very popularity of mass-produced pizzas that could undermine the future of the pizza in a relatively short time. Let me explain how.

The danger of standardization

Precisely because they are mass produced, these pizzas are characterized by an ironbound uniformity in their characteristics, especially those of flavor and appearance.

Producers can hardly escape the laws of economies of scale, and it is to their advantage to offer only a very limited number of varieties. And obviously, they are motivated to feature those varieties that market research shows are preferred by the greatest number of consumers. Moreover, for obvious competitive reasons, once the gradations of flavor and aroma preferred by most consumers for each type of pizza have been established, the food industry does everything possible to cater to those precisely researched

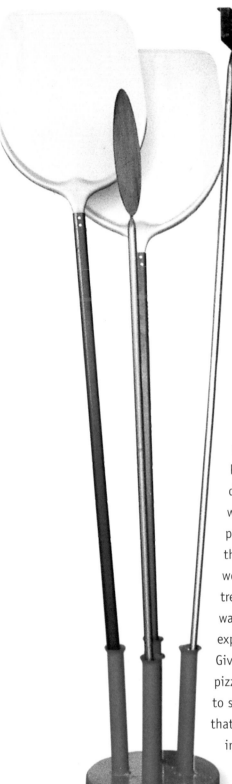

Motorcycles equipped for pizza delivery

Tools of the trade: Peels (shovels) for placing pizzas in the oven, and for turning them

preferences, creating a line of pizzas with an invariably standardized taste (though one might hope that this taste is at least the best one possible). In short, there is a risk that consumer expectation will be drastically reduced to only an extremely limited range of pizzas. And these drastically modified expectations would very likely influence what people order in a real pizzeria. In the end, pizzerias and their chefs would have to go along with the trend toward standardization if they wanted to meet their customers' expectations and stay in business. Given this scenario, the notion of pizza as a dynamic food would begin to stagnate. Over the long term, that state of affairs would lead to an inevitable decline in the pizza's evolution.

Furthermore, we should not overlook the fact that mass-produced pizzas, whether pre-packaged or sold as take-away pizza, are often consumed by families and thus will most affect the tastes and culinary habits of young people and children. For that reason, the mass-produced pizzas of today will have a considerable influence on the pizzas eaten decades from now.

A hint of optimism

These risks to the integrity of true pizza could, in fact, end up being mitigated by certain tendencies in the food industry itself. In a market with an ever-expanding pool of consumers, producers would be foolish to ignore certain pockets of market differentiation. Thus, in response to purely economic considerations, some food producers already offer pre-cooked or partially pre-cooked crusts on which the customer can build his or her own pizza at home. Who knows, we may even see product lines offered to this niche market expand to include top-quality ingredients—pre-measured, packaged, and sold individually—that allow for perfectly acceptable

pizzas to be made effortlessly at home. Given that this trend would at least provide for some degree of personalization, it is a step up from the dreary packages of pizza-in-a-box of two and three decades ago and even from many of the complete, pre-cooked, and frozen varieties now available.

Take-away pizza: back to the roots

Let me turn to another aspect of the "take-away pizza." There can be no question that the consumption of pizza has increased and continues to increase because of the growing presence of retail outlets selling this version. And that young people and chidren are among the most faithful consumers. At every hour of the day this affordably priced pizza seems to attract them in an irresistible way. But there are others who succumb to the allure of these flavorful slices of take-away pizza. All you need do is linger for a short while near one of these small retail outlets (often strategically set in crowded shopping areas) and you will soon see that a great many adults are also incapable of resisting the temptation of a short break and an invigorating snack.

And this behavior, from the point of view of anyone interested in the history of food, is especially interesting because it represents, of course, a return to the origins: the custom of eating pizza standing up, with one's hands, in a crowd—an old tradition of togetherness that seemed to have been almost lost.

Innovation: the mark of vitality

Other factors that may influence the future of the pizza are new recipe innovations. Because they are signs of vitality and creativity, new ideas are almost always accepted cordially, as long as they are not absurd or extravagant. Such ideas can lead to new developments of considerable interest. For instance, the recent practice of topping just-baked tomato-laden pizzas with fresh arugula is very exciting. Interestingly, what we have here is yet another pizza-based interpretation of a classic dish of Roman cuisine—gnocchi al pomodoro fresco e rucola, or gnocchi with fresh tomato and arugula.

Another new development is the creation of the so-called "ecological pizzeria," which

guarantees that only pizzas prepared with organically certified ingredients are served. If these establishments meet with much success, it is only a matter of time until mass-producers of food take up the idea themselves.

It is hard to guess what other innovations lie in store for us, but—as the history of pizza teaches—the imagination of pizza chefs around the world seems limitless. Do not be too surprised if, in the not-too-distant future, you are served a Pizza alle Zucchine e Gamberi, or pizza with zucchini and shrimp, with a crust fragrant with mint and, moreover, a slightly glowing pastel color thanks to the addition of finely chopped petals from one of the new species of geranium with edible petals. And don't be too amazed if you are served a Pizza alla Marinara, or seafood pizza, with a stronger aroma than usual thanks to the addition of a little fish meal to the crust. I'll let you in on an insider secret: these experiments have already been tested on a small scale, yielding perfectly acceptable results. You may soon be seeing them on the menu of your local pizzeria.

Pizza! Everyone is doing it

Another factor that could play a role in increasing the popularity of pizza is that, even more than pasta, pizza is becoming a fundamental component of that healthy and flavorful way of eating known as the "Mediterranean diet." We might go so far as to say that pizza is the "Mediterranean diet," since it provides not just the milled grains in the crust but also most of the other nourishing elements required in a healthy diet. Most people consider it as a single dish, requiring only a salad and perhaps a piece of fruit to fill it out. If the dietary completeness of true pizzas becomes better known, it could well spur the popularity of this dish even further—especially its consumption in health-conscious homes.

It certainly seems safe to predict that pizza will keep growing in popularity around the world. This will largely be due to the increasing market presence of mass-produced pre-cooked pizzas. As I've already said, this phenomenon might well result in a general standardization of the taste, smell, and appearance of the pizza.

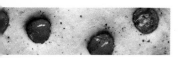

Pizza also runs the risk of undergoing a process of internationalization—a process that might well leave the pizza's culinary structure intact, at least at first, but that would obscure its origins as a dish of Italian folk cuisine. Admittedly, aside from a certain offended national pride, the phenomenon itself would be of only marginal importance, unless it engendered—over time—full-fledged mutations in the original concept of the pizza.

I imagine these predictions will be greeted with dismay by some purists, by those who will not accept the transformation of a crafts tradition into a cold industrial reality. Therefore, before moving on to explore what can be done to safeguard the quality of pizza, I think it is necessary to add a few pragmatic observations.

In the first place, we should not unfairly demonize mass-produced pizzas. Though I am loath to admit it, the food industry often has shown considerable responsibility and care in introducing pre-cooked foods. For years now, the formulation of pre-cooked dishes for mass distribution (or even for catering) has been undertaken by task forces that include highly trained chefs and reputable connoisseurs. And to be fair, mass production in the field of nutrition dates back so far that it is, in most cases, accepted without question by most everyone. Pasta, for example, which certainly forms part of the Italian culinary tradition, has been produced commercially on a large scale for almost a century, while the preserves industry has been canning peeled tomatoes since the beginning of the twentieth century. In fact, faced with the inescapable forces of consumer preference and commercial interest, there seems little that I can say that will change a thing. Think back to Cato the Censor who lived between the third and the second century BC. He used all means at his disposal to persuade the Romans to renounce leavened bread and to go back to a traditional diet, which was based—for its carbohydrates—on grain mush and unleavened cakes. The outcome? Not even a century later, millers' shops had all been converted into public bakeries and unleavened cakes had virtually vanished from the Roman daily diet.

Caricatures from a
Neapolitan pizzeria's
advertising campaign
during the G-7 summit,
Naples, 1995

Having said that, it is natural to wonder whether we can safeguard the integrity of the culinary and cultural traditions bound up with the pizza. If there is anything that can be done, what is it? Of course, the answer to the first question is definitely yes. As to what can be done, let me say that a small amount of effort can go a long way.

In my view, priority should be given to the compilation of an official collection of recipes, as complete as possible, which would also include acceptable variations on each recipe. This collection should then be regularly updated and made available to anyone who wished to consult it. As far as Italy goes, it would not be necessary to bother the Accademia

Italiana della Cucina (the Academy of Italian Cuisine), since this collection of pizza recipes could perfectly well be compiled by the *Associazione Pizzaioli Europei e Sostenitori* (A.P.E.S.). This professional association of European pizza chefs and supporters has members all over the world. The compiling and updating could be done with the cooperation of local committees, like the one recently struck in Naples, the *Associazione Vera* *Pizza Napoletana* (the association for true Neapolitan pizza). The Naples committee set about establishing a *Denominazione di Origine Controllata* system, that is, as in the wine industry, a certification that guarantees a pizza recipe's origin, the quality of its ingredients, and the method of its preparation. The idea, both in and out of Italy, might be taken so far as to have A.P.E.S.-approved pizzerias and restaurants where diners could be assured of having a true pizza made in keeping with the grand traditions of this wonderful folk dish.

Another fundamental step would be to establish a closer working collaboration between A.P.E.S. and food manufacturers, with a view to ensuring that pre-cooked pizzas comply with the classic recipes. A joint effort could be undertaken to solve technical problems in the preparation of pre-cooked pizzas, in order to safeguard the distinctive flavors and appearances of the various types of pizza. This cooperative effort should also involve the establishment of courses for the initial and ongoing training of personnel directly involved in the preparation of pre-cooked pizzas,

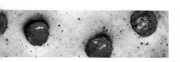

**Pizzeria in Quartzsite,
Yuma, Arizona**

including the employees of supermarkets who prepare pizzas on-site, beginning from the simple pettola right through to the baking in proper ovens.

Equally important would be an intensification of the already effective and admirable activity of A.P.E.S., an activity that should include—aside from the indispensable training courses for professional pizza chefs—seminars and conferences, open to anyone interested, as well as extensive promotional initiatives in Italy and around the world.

Pipe dreams? Perhaps. But on the other hand, what is at stake here is the future of one of the great little traditions of Italy, a tradition that is precious in historical terms and in social terms, a tradition that deserves to be nurtured and preserved over time.

A.P.E.S., THE ASSOCIATION OF PIZZA LOVERS

A.P.E.S., the *Associazione Pizzaioli Europei e Sostenitori*, literally association of European pizza chefs and supporters, was officially founded on January 26, 1981, at Giardini di Naxos in Crete. There were twenty-five charter members. A.P.E.S. was founded because, as a foodstuff, pizza was gaining immense popularity in Italy and around the world. Pizzeria after pizzeria was opening, but too often self-appointed pizza chefs with little or no training (despite their good intentions and enthusiasm) were presenting the diners crowding their premises with pizzas that did not even rise to the standard of mediocre. There were even pizza establishments that, taking their inspiration from the automatic car wash, made use of entirely automatic machinery to prepare their

pizzas, right down to the final conveyor belt trip through the tunnel oven. And amidst the increasingly cut-throat competition there was also a proliferation of new pizzas designed to attract new customers. The resulting "pizzas" often failed to adhere to the basic culinary requirements that remain the foundation of any genuine pizza. So those twenty-five charter members intended to put the brakes on all this foolishness before the pizza lost the fundamental culinary and social characteristics that had made it so popular. They feared that the pizza might turn from lovingly hand-made food, the product of ingenious folk cuisine, into a soulless industrial product.

This marked the beginning of an intense campaign for the promotion of pizza—genuine, authentic

pizza, of course—directed more at the new generation of pizza chefs than at consumers. In close collaboration with Italian hotels and trade schools, professional courses covered not only the art of making pizza, but also the history of that art, so as to give the chefs a sense of the heritage that was in danger of being lost. As time went on, the courses improved considerably. They now include the fundamentals on which drinks go with which pizzas, and how the pizzas and drinks should be served. In order to engender a sense of pride, the official Albo dei Pizzaioli Europei (Registry of European Pizza Chefs) was established. Membership in the Albo is unrestricted, but only professional chefs who belong to the Albo are eligible to participate in the annual pizza competi-

tion that A.P.E.S. holds. The winner is awarded the prestigious title of "Primo Pizzaiolo d'Europa"—the top pizza chef of all Europe.

A.P.E.S. also established a newsletter, and in honor of the many pizza chefs working in the United States, the newsletter is called *Pizza-Press*. The current editor-in-chief (and founder) is Antonio Primiceri, one of the charter members of A.P.E.S. Antonio is not only a pizza chef, but also the son of a pizza chef who runs the family restaurant/pizzeria in Milan. The newsletter helps promote A.P.E.S. events that are now increasingly aimed at consumers. In fact, A.P.E.S. has also become a major purchasing group. It ensures its members excellent products and ingredients at reasonable prices—and, best of all, pizza lovers are the ultimate beneficiaries of this arrangement.

While most of the activities I describe are in Italy, I hope that these might serve as a model for the promotion and preservation of pizza the world over, either through A.P.E.S. or other regional food bodies that are concerned about the integrity of culinary traditions. That said, the activities of A.P.E.S. extend over at least five continents and we should all be grateful for the worthwhile service being offered by this organization. This association safeguards the original and distinctive qualities of the pizza for those of us around the world who love true pizzas and pizzerias.

Pizzapress, the newsletter of A.P.E.S.

APPENDICES

Pizza

Quattro Stagioni	Capricciosa	Diavola	Quattro Formaggi	Funghi Porcini	Prosciutto e Funghi	Melanzane	Pescatora	Zucchine e Gamberi	Tonno	Anguilla	Tedesca	Pizza with Sausages	Gorgonzola e Ananas
82	84	86	88	90	92	94	96	98	100	102	104	106	108

Notes on the ingredients

1. **Anchovies**
   You should use the classic, rather large variety, preserved in salt, rinsed and patted dry. You can also use anchovy filets in oil after thoroughly draining the oil.

2. **Artichokes**
   Best if fresh. The important thing is to eliminate the hard outer leaves and any fuzz on the heart itself. You can also use frozen artichokes, as long as they are in segments, or good-quality bottled or canned artichoke hearts, drained.

3. **Basil**
   You should use very fresh basil with large fleshy leaves. Or use dried whole basil leaves.

4. **Black olives**
   The variety, of course, depends on personal preference, but the simpler the better. Remember to pit them first.

5. **Caciocavallo**
   This strong-flavored cheese from southern Italy should be savory but not salty; spicy but not excessively so. The question of age depends on what kind of pizza you want—mild or bold—and your own personal tastes. Smoked mozzarella or smoked provolone (or unsmoked) may be used as they are of the same family of cheeses.

6. **Calamint (also known as nepitella)**
   A mellow mint used by Italians for generations to flavor vegetables. It tastes like a mild mint with a hint of oregano. It grows wild in Italy. If not available, use equal parts regular mint and fresh oregano.
   Note: Large amounts of certain calamints have been known to cause miscarriages; to be absolutely safe, pregnant women should avoid all varieties.

7. **Capers**
   If you have the choice, pick medium-sized capers. If they are packed in brine, drain and leave in cold water for an hour, and then drain again. If pickled, rinse well before using.

8. **Capasanta, or pilgrim scallops (scallops)**
   This is a distinctive variety of shellfish that, in Italy, is cooked with or without the pink coral roe. Its exquisite, fine flavor is best reserved for the simplest of treatments. Substitute large, fresh sea scallops, with or without roe, as you wish.

9. **Clams**
   Best if they are fresh and large, but frozen clams or clams preserved in brine are also acceptable. Be sure to drain the liquid thoroughly.

10. **Eel**
    The outcome of the Pizza all'Anguilla (Pizza with Smoked Eel) depends on the quality of the eel, as well as the size of the fillets, which should not be too thick and—especially—should have the right degree of softness. Since eel is difficult to find in North America, you can use another rich, thick-fleshed fish of your choice, or a smoked fish, either haddock or cod.

11. **Eggplants**
    Use either conventional eggplant, globe (also known as Sicilian) eggplant or the slender, purple Asian (or Japanese) eggplant. Whichever variety you choose, keep slices of uniform thickness.

12. **Flour**
    Traditionally, this should be a white flour made from durum wheat, but any good unbleached, all-purpose baking flour is perfectly acceptable. If you want to approximate a version of the Italian "00" flour ("dopio zero") for the pizzas, combine one part pastry flour with three parts all-purpose flour.

13. Frankfurters

Look for good quality German-style wurst. Chicken or turkey frankfurters are acceptable as well as the beef. The important thing is that the diameter be no less than about 1 inch (2 or 3 cm).

14. Garlic

The garlic should be as fresh as possible, and should always be used sparingly. Its aroma should blend with those of the other ingredients, not overwhelm them.

15. Gherkins

Drain these pickles well before using them. Even though you'll chop them up, don't do it too finely; this way, they retain a pleasant softness.

16. Gorgonzola cheese

For pizza, creamy gorgonzola is better than the drier variety, which is generally a bit too strong.

17. Ham

Do not use smoked hams.

18. Formaggelle, or small fresh cheeses

Depending on personal taste, use both ricotta and fresh tomino. Tomino is an unpasteurized full-fat or partly-skimmed cow's milk cheese, produced in Piedmont, the Aosta Valley, and Liguria. It has the soft, mellow flavors of cheeses rich in pasture-land. If not available, use a mild young cheese, a mozzarella, or a mild goat's cheese. Do not use feta cheese, which is too sharp for the Migliaciti recipe, and avoid the "formaggi bianchi extramagri," or skim milk white cheeses, which, on the other hand, would add nothing to the overall flavor.

19. Lard or lardo

While not especially popular with North Americans, lard in some form has long been used in Italians cooking. If you wish, you may substitute another fat in its place.

20. Luganega

This is a long, thin fresh pork sausage made of slightly coarse ground pork with a 40% fat content. A specialty of the North-ern and Central regions of Italy, it is often eaten with tomato sauce alongside a serving of polenta during the cold months. Use a good quality pork sausage, with or without garlic, as a substitute.

21. Mint

Be careful not to use too much, lest its aroma overwhelm the other scents; we recommend using fresh leaves, but dried leaves also give excellent results.

22. Mozzarella

When pizza was first invented, the mozzarella was made with "latte di bufala," or buffalo milk. Nowadays, in part to satisfy the enormous and growing demand, mozzarella is also made with ordinary cow's milk. If you cannot find the original "moz-zarella di bufala," the ordinary type will do just fine. In any case, for a good pizza you must use only the freshest mozzarel-la—it should be very soft, pliable (without being rubbery), and not very watery. Before you cut it up into little cubes, squeeze it in your hand to eliminate any excess moisture.

23. Mushrooms

The Pizza al Prosciutto e ai Funghi (Pizza with Prosciutto and Mushrooms) was developed specifically for regular white button mushrooms, but any kind of fresh mushrooms can be used, depending on personal tastes and availability. You can also obtain good results with dried mushrooms, as long as they are of good quality. Make sure to follow package directions for rehydrat-ing properly.

24. Mussels

It is best to use fresh mussels, but you can also use frozen mussels or mussels preserved in brine, if available. In the latter case, drain thoroughly.

25. Olive oil

When pizza was first invented, there were only two kinds of olive oil: good and bad. Nowadays chefs tend to use extra virgin olive oil when making pizza. All the same, since pizza is baked at high temperatures, any good olive oil will do, as long as it is low in acidity.

26. Onions

Red onions—with a rounded flavor and gentle aroma—yield the best results, especially if you remove the bitterish outer layers and slice the rest thinly and evenly.

27. Oregano

If it is of high quality and reasonably fresh, oregano has a pleasant and strong aroma, so you should never use too much.

28. Parsley

Of course, the best thing is to use fresh parsley—Italian flat-leaf or curly.

29. Parmesan cheese

This can be replaced with any good "grana padano," as long as it has been properly aged. "Grana padano" is made in the same way as Parmigiano Reggiano, but not aged as long. It may be used in exactly the same way as Parmigiano Reggiano, but is slightly different in flavor and slightly less expensive than the regal Parmigiano Reggiano.

30. Pecorino cheese

This sheep's milk cheese needs to be properly aged. The quantity used should vary according to how long and how well the cheese has been aged, where the cheese is from and, of course, your personal preferences. If it is absolutely impossible to find pecorino, you can use a well-aged caciocavallo (see above) or else a well-aged (but not smoked) sheep's milk ricotta.

31. Peppers

Red, green, yellow, or orange bell peppers may be used. These should be meaty and flavorful; be careful not to use spicy ones.

32. Pineapple

Always use fresh, ripe pineapples if possible; many supermarkets now sell pre-peeled pineapple in containers. Cut away all the tough woody parts near the rind and the central core. Or, use good-quality canned pineapple, well drained.

33. Porcini mushrooms

If possible, the mushrooms should be fresh, but dried mushrooms can be used to make excellent pizza. (See Mushrooms, above.)

34. Prosciutto

Try to use "Original Prosciutto" from Italy. It should be sliced fairly thick, and it's best if a bit of fat is left on it. If not, after baking, the prosciutto can take on an unpleasant parchment-like consistency.

35. Provola

This is a typical cheese from southern Italy, but it's difficult to find a substitute. In a pinch, you could try a young Dutch Gouda or provolone.

36. Provola Affumicata, or smoked provola

This is a delicately smoked provola for which a substitute is difficult to find. You could try smoked provolone or smoked mozzarella.

37. Red chili pepper
The best results are had by grinding whole, dried red chili peppers. Wash your hands well after handling.

38. Robiola
This is a full-cream, unaged cheese, ranging from soft to creamy, with a delicate flavor. It's typical of northern Italy and can be replaced with any comparable cheese, such as good-quality farmer's cheese or a solid cream cheese.

39. Rosemary
For Focaccia/Pizza Bianca (White Pizza), the rosemary should be absolutely fresh.

40. Salame al Peperoncino (pepperoni) or salami with red chili pepper
It is best to use a fine-grained salami, and the salami should be no more than 2 to 2½ inches (5 or 6 cm) in diameter; the presence of garlic is not a problem.

41. Salami
Here, too, the grain should be quite fine, with a diameter no less than 2 inches (5 cm).

42. Sausage
Let personal tastes guide you here. Lean, quality sausage made of beef, pork, or veal, or a combination, is best. Also, those with a base of red wine, garlic, and cheese will provide extra flavor.

43. Scamorza
Scamorza is a cheese made in the same tradition as mozzarella. It is a young, fresh-tasting cheese. Substitute a young or soft mozzarella.

44. Shrimp
Fresh or frozen shrimps are excellent, the important thing being that they are medium sized. This prevents them from becoming stringy during baking.

45. Speck
Speck is a smoked, salt-cured, air-dried ham made from pork shoulder. It is originally an Austrian specialty so will be available at many German or European delis or butchershops. If you can find a smoked pancetta (Italian bacon), it may also be used.

46. Stracchino
This is a semi-fatty unaged cheese, ranging from soft to creamy, with a delicate flavor, typical of northern Italy. It can be replaced with any comparable cheese, such as mild fontina, provided that it has no acid or bitter taste or aftertaste.

47. Tomatoes
If you can, use San Marzano tomatoes, or good-quality canned Italian plum tomatoes, drained. The important thing is that they be meaty, with a low water content. Always make sure they are peeled and eliminate the seeds if you can.

48. Tomato sauce
The sauce recipe given here has been adapted to North American preferences. If you like, you may replace it with an Italian tomato and basil sauce, but it must be quite dense.

49. Tuna
Any canned tuna is acceptable, packed in either water or olive oil. Before using it, of course, you should drain the liquid.

50. Zucchini and Zucchini blossoms
Use either green or yellow zucchini. Make sure to slice them evenly.

Index of pizzas

Page numbers in bold type refer to recipes.

Index of wines

Picture credits

Agenzia ADNA
82, 114, 115, 117, 124

Agenzia Contrasto
Keith Bernstein/IPG 152
Enrico Bossan 26-27, 49, 51, 53t
Rosen/Saba/Rea 131bl
Saba/Rea 53b
Slakely/Saba/Rea 131br
Shobha 131cr
Charles Worth 131tr

Agenzia Reporter Press
135

Archivio Farabolafoto
21, 25, 131tl-cl, 132, 133
Bianchi 131
Jovane 149

Archivio Fotografico SCALA
33, 34, 37

Centro Documentazione Mondadori
19, 43, 45, 47, 54, 72, 90, 92, 135t

Roberto Della Noce
8b, 22, 24, 143 cr-bl-br, 145tl-tr-bl-br

Maj-Britt Idström
from 2 to 9, 15, 16, 17, 62, 64, 80, 94, 96, 100, 108,
and all of the odd-numbered pages from 59 to 109

Massimo Mazzilli
1, 10, 14, 15, 17, 38, 39, 68, 84, 88, 104, 120, 121,
122, 123, 125, 127, 134, 135c-b, 136, 137, 138b,
139, 140, 141, 143, 145cl-cr-bc, 146/147

Ubik-Maurizio Lodi
41, 61, 86, 116, 118, 138t, 150

The numbers refer to the pages; the abbreviations t,
b, c, r, l, refer to the location of the illustration on
the page (top, bottom, center, right, left).